AF351094

Publisher's Note

While not as well known as many of Spurgeon's other titles, I'm glad *John Ploughman's Talk* can still today be enjoyed by young and old alike. I love Spurgeon's wit and wisdom as he plainly addresses everything from our need for Christ, to everyday "respectable sins."

We opted to keep the original illustrations in this classic, and even touched up and reused the original cover image. We also kept the blue canvas look for the cover background, to closely mirror the early editions.

I trust you will be challenged, encouraged, and even humored as you read this old, yet fresh, volume. May the Lord continually instruct, bless, and keep you as you travel the narrow path.

In Christ,
Jeremiah Zeiset
Publisher, Aneko Press

John Ploughman's Talk

Register This New Book

Benefits of Registering*

- ✓ FREE **replacements** of lost or damaged books

- ✓ FREE **audiobook** – *Pilgrim's Progress*, audiobook edition

- ✓ FREE information about new titles and other **freebies**

www.anekopress.com/new-book-registration

*See our website for requirements and limitations.

John Ploughman's Talk

Plain Advice for Plain People

ANEKO PRESS

John Ploughman's Talk

© 2025 by Aneko Press

All rights reserved. First edition 1896.

Revisions copyright 2025.

Please do not reproduce, store in a retrieval system, or transmit in any form or by any means – electronic, mechanical, photocopying, recording, or otherwise, without written permission from the publisher.

Scripture quotations from The Authorized (King James) Version. Rights in the Authorized Version in the United Kingdom are vested in the Crown. Reproduced by permission of the Crown's patentee, Cambridge University Press.

Editor: C. Miskimen

Aneko Press

www.anekopress.com

Aneko Press, Life Sentence Publishing, and our logos are trademarks of

Life Sentence Publishing, Inc.
203 E. Birch Street
P.O. Box 652
Abbotsford, WI 54405

RELIGION / Christian Living / Spiritual Growth

Paperback ISBN: 979-8-88936-529-7

eBook ISBN: 979-8-88936-530-3

10   9   8   7   6   5   4   3   2   1

Available where books are sold

Contents

Preface

I have written *John Ploughman's Talk* for working folk – ploughmen and plain people. So I have left out flowery words and refined tastes on purpose and instead have chosen to use strong sayings and everyday expressions. I have taken aim at common vices and tried to teach moral values that all men need.

Many things that the working class needs to hear are not suitable for the pulpit on a Sunday morning. My hope is that these humble pages teach thrift and hard work every day of the week, both at home and in the workshop. If even just a few people learn these lessons, I will not regret using this plain and simple style.

Ploughman is a name I can rightly lay claim to. Every minister has put his hand to the plough to break up the fallow ground of men's hearts. I do not feel I need to apologize for writing in a semi-humorous style. It has helped over 300,000 people hear sound moral teaching. There is no special virtue in being serious and unreadable.

I saw a jar that said, "If you like our pickles, try our sauce." Well, then, if you enjoy *John Ploughman's Talk,* also take a look at *John Ploughman's Pictures*, a second volume written in the same character as this.

C. H. Spurgeon

To the Idle

It's no more use giving advice to an idle man than pouring water into a sieve – and trying to improve one is about as hopeful as trying to fatten a greyhound. But since the Good Book tells us to *cast your bread upon the waters* (Ecclesiastes 11:1), we will toss a hard crust or two on these stagnant ponds. Lazy fellows may not improve, but we'll be none the worse for warning them. When you sow good sense, your basket stays full.

We have some dense soil to plough when we try to chide sluggards, and the crop will be small. But if only good land were farmed, ploughmen would be out of work, so we'll put the plough into the furrow. Idle men grow like weeds, without planting, but the amount of wit among seven acres of them would not even pay to rake them up. Their name and character is enough to prove this; if they were not fools, they would not be idlers.

Laziness is in some people's bones and will show itself in their idle flesh no matter what you do to them.

Solomon said, *The sluggard is wiser in his own conceit than seven men that can render a reason* (Proverbs 26:16), but to everyone else, his folly shines like the sun in the sky. If I speak sharply to them, it is because I know they can take it. If I had them down on the old barn floor, I could thresh them all day and still not get them out of the straw. Even a steam thresher could not do it. They would let it kill them before they would get up. Laziness is in some people's bones and will show itself in their idle flesh no matter what you do to them.

First off, it strikes me that lazy people ought to have a large mirror hung up in their cottages where they would be sure to see themselves in it. If their eyes are at all like mine, they could not bear to look at themselves long or often. The ugliest sight in all the world is one of those thoroughbred loafers who would not hold up his bowl if it were to rain porridge. For certain, he would never hold up a bigger pot so he could give to others. Perhaps, if the porridge turned to beer, he might wake himself up a bit, but he would make up for it afterward with a nap.

This is the lazy man in the Proverbs, who *buries his hand in the bowl; it wearies him to bring it back to his mouth* (Proverbs 26:15). Men like this ought to be treated like drones that the bees drive out of the hives. Every man should pity the poor but take a long whip to the lazy – or a turn at the treadmill might be better. This would be good medicine for all sluggards, but some of them will never get their full dose of this medicine because they were born with silver spoons in their mouths – and like spoons, they cannot stir their own tea unless somebody lends them a hand. They are, as the old saying goes, *as lazy as Ludlam's dog* – who leaned his head against the wall to bark. Like lazy sheep, they find it too much trouble to carry their own wool. If they could see their reflection, it might by chance do them a world of good, but most likely it would be too much trouble for them to open their eyes even if the mirror were hung for them.

Everything in the world is of some use, but it would puzzle a doctor of divinity, a philosopher, or the wisest owl in our steeple to tell me the good of idleness. That's an ill wind that blows no good, a mud where eels won't breed, a dirty ditch with no food for a frog. Sift a sluggard grain by grain, and you'll find nothing but chaff.

I have heard men say, "Better to do nothing than do mischief," but I am not sure of that. The saying glitters well, but I don't believe it's gold. I will not give laziness even that pinch of praise – it is bad and bad altogether.

A man doing wrong is a sparrow eating corn, but a lazy man is a sparrow sitting on a nest full of eggs – they will soon hatch and do a lot more harm. The foulest weeds on earth don't grow in the minds of those who are busy at wickedness but in the foul corners of idle minds – where the devil can hide unseen like the old serpent he is.

I would even rather that our boys were up to their necks in mud than sauntering around with nothing to do. Laziness may look harmless today, but it will grow into full-grown sin tomorrow. The devil is putting coals on the fire. There is no blaze yet, but it is warming up and will be a bigger fire in the end.

Idle people, you need to be your own trumpeters, for no one else has anything good to say about you. I'd rather see you through a telescope than anything else – you would at least be a long way off – but even if we used the strongest pair of spectacles we could find, we would not be able to see anything in you worth talking about. There's something to be said for moles, rats, and weasels – even though there are plenty of them nailed up on our old barn – they can at times be useful. But as for you – your only usefulness is in the grave to help make the churchyard bigger.

Here's the best thing I can say about you – it is a little rhyme of my own:

A good-for-nothing lazy lout,
Wicked within and ragged without,
Who can bear to have him about?
Turn him out! Turn him out!

As vinegar to the teeth and smoke to the eyes (Proverbs 10:26) is the sluggard to every man who sweats to earn an honest living while these fellows let the grass grow up to their ankles, standing around using up the ground, as the Bible says (Luke 13:7).

A lazy man makes himself a target for the devil, who is a wonderfully good rifleman. Idle men tempt the devil to tempt them. The man who plays when he should work has an evil spirit for his playmate. He who neither works nor plays is a workshop for Satan. If the devil catches a man idle, he will give him a job, find him tools, and before long, pay him wages.

A lazy man makes himself a target for the devil.

Isn't this where drunkenness and ruin begin? Laziness is the key to beggary and the root of all evil. Fellows have two stomachs for eating and drinking when they have no stomach for work. That little hole just under the nose swallows up in idle hours the money that should have put clothes on the children's backs and bread on the cottage table. God's Word tells us: *the drunkard and the glutton will come to poverty*; and to show the connection between them. The same verse adds: *and drowsiness will clothe a man with rags* (Proverbs 23:21). Just as I know that moss grows on an old thatch roof, I know that drunkenness and irresponsibility grow out of lazy hours.

I like leisure when I can get it, but that's a different thing – one is cheese and the other chalk. Idle folks don't know what leisure is. They are always behind, always in a hurry, and always a mess. By neglecting to work at the proper time, they always have a lot to do. Lolling about hour after hour, with nothing to do, is just making holes in the hedge to let the pigs through.

And the pigs will come through. Make no mistake – nobody knows better the rooting and damage they will do than those who have to look after the garden. Jesus Himself said when *men slept, the enemy came and sowed tares* (Matthew 13:25). That hits the nail on the head, for evil enters the heart most often through the door of sluggishness.

Our old minister used to say, "A sluggard is fine raw material for the devil. He can make anything he likes out of him – from a thief right up to a murderer."

I'm not the only one who condemns the idle, for once, when I was going to give our minister a pretty long list of the sins of one of our people that he was checking on, I began with, "He's dreadfully lazy."

"That's enough," said the old gentleman. "All sorts of sins are in that one. That's how you know a full-fledged sinner."

I've always warned my boys: "Stay out of the sluggard's way or you may catch his disease and never get rid of it." I am always afraid that they might learn the ways of the idle, so I watch for signs of laziness in them and try to nip them in the bud – it's best to kill a lion while it's a cub. Sure enough, our children have our evil nature in them, for you can see it growing by itself like weeds in a garden.

Who can bring a clean thing out of the unclean? A wild goose never lays a tame egg. If we don't make a green and lively space for them at home, our boys will wander off to the village green to join the loafers. Train them to hate the company of the slothful. Never let them go to The Rose and Crown – or any other pub. Let them learn to earn a crown while they are young and grow the roses in their father's garden at home. Raise bees, not drones.

People complain about bad masters these days – and I do not doubt there's some truth in it – but there is plenty to complain against the working people too, especially about this matter of slothfulness. We have to plough with the oxen we have, but when I get teamed up to work with some men, I'd rather drive a team of snails or go out rabbit hunting with a dead ferret. Why, you'd sooner get blood out of a gatepost or juice out of a cork than work out of some of them. Yet they are always talking about their *rights*. I wish they would look to their *wrongs* and not lean on the plough handles. Lazy lie-a-beds aren't working men any more than pigs are bulls or thistles are apple trees.

Not everyone in a red coat is a hunter, and not everyone in work clothes is a worker. I wonder, sometimes, why some of our employers keep so many cats who catch no mice. I'd just as soon drop my wages down a well as pay some people for pretending to work. It makes your flesh crawl to watch them move all day like a slug creeping over a cabbage leaf. "Live and let live," I say, but I don't include sluggards in that saying. If a man won't work, neither let him eat (2 Thessalonians 3:10).

Here, perhaps, is the proper place to say that some of the higher classes, as they are called, set a shamefully bad example in this respect: Many of the rich are as lazy as they are wealthy – maybe more so. The big dormice sleep as long and as sound as the little ones.

There are preachers who buy or borrow a sermon to save themselves the trouble of thinking. That is just abominable laziness. The Ranters they sneer at would be ashamed to stand up and read somebody else's sermon as if it were his own.[1] Many of our squires have nothing to do but to part their hair in the middle, and many of the grand people of London, I am told, have no better work than killing time.

Now, they say the higher a monkey climbs, the more his tail is seen, and so, the greater these people are, the more their idleness is noticed and the more they ought to be ashamed of it. I don't say they all need to work the plough, but I do say that they ought to do something useful for the state. Right now, they are like caterpillars on the cabbage, eating up the good things or like butterflies, showing themselves off but making no honey. I cannot be angry with these people somehow, for I pity them when I think of the stupid rules of fashion they are forced to follow and the emptiness in which they weary out their days. I'd sooner break my back with hard work than have nothing to do but look in the mirror all day at a fellow who never put a single potato into the nation's pot but took a good many out. Let me drop dead on these Surrey hills, worn out like my master's old brown mare, sooner than eat bread and cheese I didn't earn. It's better to die an honorable death than live a good-for-nothing life.

---

1   In the mid-1600s, the Ranters were a religious group characterized by mystical and antinomian beliefs, but by Spurgeon's day, "Ranters" was a term usually applied to Primitive Methodists because of their more boisterous preaching and worship services.

Still, lazy people don't get off so easy in the end. They skip patching the roof and end up having to rebuild the house. They will not put the horse in the cart, so they have to drag it themselves. If they were wise, they would do their work well and get the job done right the first time – and tug hard while they are in harness to get the work out of the way. My advice is, if you hate hard work, just get on with it and get it finished so you can take a proper rest.

If you hate hard work, just get on with it and get it finished so you can take a proper rest.

I wish more religious folk would take this matter to heart. Some so-called Christians are amazingly lazy and give the tongues of the wicked something to do. A godly ploughman ought to be the best man in the field, and no team should outwork him. When it is time to work, work – don't stop the plough to chat, even if the chat is about religion. That wastes not only your employer's time, but the time of the horses too. I used to hear people say, "Never stop the plough to catch a mouse," and it's just as foolish to stop for idle chat. The man who slacks off when the master is away is an eye-server (Colossians 3:22), which, I take it, is the very opposite of a Christian.

If more of our members were a little quicker with their arms and legs at work and a little slower with their tongues, they would speak more for the faith than they do now. The world says the worst rogue is the pious rogue, and I'm sorry to say one of the laziest men I know is a professing Christian of the "Mr. Talkative" kind. His garden is so overgrown with weeds that I have half a mind to weed it myself just to save our church the shame he brings on it. If he were a young lad, I'd talk to him about it and try to teach him better, but what can you do with a sixty-year-old child?

He is a thorn in our pastor's side. The poor minister often says he'll move somewhere else to get away from him, but I tell him that wherever a man lives he is sure to have one thornbush near his door, and it is a mercy if there are not two. Still, I do wish all Christians would be hard workers. Religion was never designed to make us idle. Jesus was a tireless worker, and His disciples must not be afraid of hard work.

As for serving God with cold hearts and drowsy souls, we have had way too much of that. It causes religion to wither. Men ride stags when they are chasing money but snails on the road to heaven. Preachers drone on, and the people yawn, fold their arms, and doze and then say that God is withholding the blessing. A sluggard who finds himself in a disorganized, ragged regiment blames his luck. Some churches have learned the same wicked excuse. I believe that when Paul plants and Apollos waters, God gives the increase. If there is no harvest, the blame is with us, not Him.

Well, that's the end of my rope. Maybe I have been watering a dead stump, but I have done my best – and a king can do no more. An ant can never make honey even if it works its heart out, and I'll never put my thoughts together pretty like some do, all book-fashion. But truth is still truth, even when dressed in homespun. And with that, I've said my piece.

On Religious Grumblers

"No piper ever played a tune that pleased every ear." – Page 15

When a man has a particularly empty head, he usually sets himself up as a great judge – especially in matters of religion. There's no one quite so confident as the fellow who knows nothing. His ignorance is the mother of his arrogance and the nurse of his stubbornness. Though he can't tell B from a bull's foot, he talks as though all wisdom was at his fingertips. Why, the pope himself could scarcely be more infallible!

Listen to him after he's been to a meeting and heard a sermon – you'll learn how to tear down a good man if you didn't already know. He sees faults where there are none, and if there a few small blemishes, he turns every mouse into an elephant. You could fit all his wisdom into an eggshell, yet he weighs the sermon in the scales of his conceit like he was as wise as King Solomon. If the sermon met his standards, he slathers on his praise with a trowel; but if not, he growls and barks and snaps like a dog at a hedgehog.

Faultfinders find fault with anything and nothing.

Wise men in this world are like trees in a hedge – there is one only here and there. When these rare men get together and talk about a sermon, it's worth listening in. But the bragging know-it-alls are all puffed up, and their fault-finding makes as much sense as the sound of geese honking on the village green. Nothing comes out of a sack but what is in it, and since their sack is empty, they shake out nothing but hot air.

Of course, no minister or sermon is perfect – even the best garden may have a few weeds in it, and the cleanest corn may have some chaff. But faultfinders find fault with anything and nothing. They find fault for the sake of showing off their deep knowledge. Sooner than let their tongues have a holiday, they would complain that the grass is not a nice shade of blue and say that the sky would have looked neater if it had been whitewashed.

One tribe of these Ishmaelites is made up of puffed-up ignoramuses who are most mighty in their own minds about "sound doctrine." In this matter, they are as decisive as sledgehammers and as certain as death. He who knows nothing is confident in everything, so they are bullheaded beyond measure. Every clock – even the sundial – must be set according to their watches, and the slightest difference from their opinion proves a man is rotten at heart. Argue with them, and their little pot boils over in quick style. Ask them for reason, and you might as well go to a sandpit for sugar.

They think they have bottled up the sea of truth and carry it in their waistcoat pockets. They have measured out the exact length of God's electing love and tied a knot in the string to prove it. As for the deep things of God that angels long to know, they claim to have seen them all – like boys gawking at peep shows at the fair. Having sold their modesty and become wiser than their teachers, they ride a very high horse and leap right over any Bible text that teaches contrary to their notions.

When this nonsense creeps into good men, it's a pity to see such sweet ointment spoiled by flies. Still, I learn to bear with them just as I do with old Violet, my horse. He is a remarkable horse, even if he does set his ears back and throw out his legs and kick at times. But there is a black-hearted crowd around who are all sting and no honey, all whip and no hay, all grunt and no bacon. They do nothing but rant and complain from morning to night at anyone who cannot see through their spectacles.

If only they would mix in a handful of good works

with all their bushels of bluster, it might be bearable. But no, they are too spiritual for that. Men as sound as they are can't be expected to be good at anything else. They are the heavenly watchdogs to guard the house of the Lord from those thieves and robbers who don't preach sound doctrine. If they do worry the sheep or steal a rabbit or two on the sly, who's to blame them? The Lord's "dear" people, as they call themselves, have enough to do to keep their doctrine sound, so it's no wonder that their manners are a little off – no one can see to everything at once.

These are the moles that need caught in many of our pastures – not for their own sakes, for there is not a sweet mouthful in them – but for the sake of the meadows that they spoil. I could overlook their doctrine if they had a better spirit, but vinegar is sweet to it, and crabs are figs in comparison. I'll take strong doctrine any day, but I want high experience and holy living to go with it, or else it turns my stomach. However, I have had my say and must leave the subject, or somebody will ask me, "What have you to do with Bradshaw's wind mill?"[2]

Sometimes it is not what the preacher says, but *how* he says it that gets raked over the coals. Here again is a wide field for nitpicking. Every bean has its black, and every man has his failing. Every good horse has some odd habit or other, and I never yet saw a minister worth his salt who did not have some whimsey or oddity. And these are the very things the faultfinders sniff

---

2   This question is asked of a character in Charles Dickens' novel Hard Times. In modern language, we might say, "Why are you wasting your time with that?"

out and gnaw on. One man is too slow, and another too fast. The first is too flowery, and the second is too dull.

Dear me, if we judged all God's creatures this way, we would wring the dove's neck for being too tame, shoot the robins for eating spiders, kill the cows for swinging their tails and the hens for not giving us milk. A man looking to beat a dog can always find a stick, and by this standard, any fool could criticize the best minister in England.

As to a preacher's manner – if it's plain and earnest, that is good enough. No man should use bad language in the pulpit – and all language is bad that common people cannot make head or tail of. No one should complain about godly, sober, decent, and plain words. A countryman is as warm in cotton as a king in velvet, and a truth is as comfortable in humble words as in fine speech. Hungry men leave it to the cook to stir and serve the meat – their only care is that it is sweet and substantial.

If the listeners were better, sermons would be better. When men say they can't hear, I recommend they buy a hearing horn and remember the old saying, *There's none so deaf as those who will not hear.*

When young preachers get discouraged because of hard, unkind remarks, I generally tell them of the old man, the boy, and the donkey and what came of trying to please everybody.[3] No piper ever played a tune that pleased every ear. Where whims and fancies sit in the seat of judgment, a man's opinion is only so much

---

3   This is referring to one of Aesop's fables in which he highlights the vanity of trying to please everyone. Their attempts led to the donkey's death.

wind. Therefore, take no more notice of it than of the wind whistling through a keyhole.

Some folks find fault with a sermon not for what *was* said, but for what *wasn't*. No matter how well the subject was handled, there was another subject about which nothing was said, so the whole thing was useless.

This is as sensible as finding fault with my ploughing because it does make the holes for the beans or abusing a good corn field because there are no turnips in it. Does any man look for every truth in one sermon? You might as well look for every dish at one meal, and scold a beef roast because there was no bacon, veal, peas, or parsnips on the table.

Suppose a sermon is not full of comfort for the saint, but it warned the sinner – should we hate it? A handsaw would be a poor tool to shave with, so should we throw it away? What is the use of always trying to hunt out faults? Some people go around sniffing for things to complain about like a ratcatcher's dog sniffing at rat holes. By all means, chop down error, root and branch, but let's save our blades until there are brambles to chop and not fall victim to our own judgment.

Judging preachers is a poor trade. Nobody gets paid for it, and nobody profits by it. At a ploughing match, at least the best man wins a prize, but these critics of preaching are precious slow to give anything, even to the ones they claim to admire. They pay in cheap praise but give no pudding. They get the gospel for nothing, and if they do not grumble, think that they have paid pretty well.

Everybody thinks he is a good judge of a sermon, but nine out of ten might as well pretend to weigh the moon. Most people think preaching is easy and they could do it better themselves. Every donkey thinks it is worthy to stand with the king's horses; every girl thinks she could keep house better than her mother. But thoughts are not facts. The sprat thought itself a herring, but the fisherman knew better.

Some men can whistle fancy and think that qualifies them to plough, but there's more to being a good ploughman than whistling. And there's more to good preaching than taking a text, and saying, "first, second, and third." I try my hand at preaching myself, and it is no easy thing to give the folks something worth hearing, and if the fine critics, who pass judgment so easily, would try it themselves, they might pipe down a bit.

> **It is a dreadful thing to see a happy church of Christians broken up by talkative faultfinders.**

Dogs, however, will always bark, and what is worse, some of them will bite too. But decent people ought to do all they can to muzzle them or at least prevent them from doing any great mischief.

It is a dreadful thing to see a happy church of Christians broken up by talkative faultfinders, and all about nothing or less than nothing. A small wedge in the devil's hands can split apart a church. The fact is, the worst wheel of the cart makes the most noise, and one fool makes many more. That's how a good and faithful minister is run off by the people who needed his care and friendship the most.

Those who are at the root of the mischief are usually those who have no part in true godliness. Like sparrows, they fight over corn that is not theirs, or like jackdaws, they pull down what they never helped to build.

From mad dogs and grumbling church members, may we all be delivered. And may we never catch the disease they carry. Fault-finding is contagious: one dog will set a whole kennel howling, and the wisest course is to keep out of the way of a man who has the spiritual grumbles.

The worst part is that the foot and mouth disease go together: he who throws mud at others eventually rolls in the mud himself. *The fruit of the Spirit is love* (Galatians 5:22) – and that fruit looks nothing like the sour crabapples some people bring. Farewell, all you complainers! John Ploughman would rather gnaw on a bone in peace than fight over a whole roasted ox.

On the Preacher's Appearance

"You cannot judge a horse by his harness." – Page 22

A good horse doesn't have to be a certain color, and a truly good preacher can wear what he pleases – few will care. Still, though you cannot judge wine by the barrel, a respectable appearance is a letter of recommendation, even to a ploughman.

Wise men don't fall in love or take offense at first sight, but even they say a first impression is a good thing. As for those weaker sort who are not wise, a good appearance is half the battle.

What do I mean by a good appearance? Well, it's not being pompous and stiff or acting high and mighty among the people. Pride loses hearts, and gentle words win them. It's not wearing fine clothes either. Foppish clothing often hides a repulsive house within – even with a whitewashed doorstep without. Such dressing tells the world that the outside is the best part of the puppet. When a man is proud as a peacock, all strut and show, he needs to be converted himself before he begins to preach to others. The preacher who measures himself by his mirror may please a few silly girls, but neither God nor man will put up with him for long.

The man who owes his greatness to his tailor will find that needle and thread won't hold a fool in the pulpit. A gentleman should have more in his pocket than on his back, and a minister should have more in his heart than on his coat.

I'd say to young preachers – don't preach in gloves. Cats in mittens catch no mice. Don't curl and oil your hair like a peacock because nobody comes to hear a peacock's voice. Don't fill your thoughts with how you look at all, or no one else will pay attention to you.

Don't wear gold rings, chains, or jewelry. The pulpit is

no place for a jewelry shop. Forever do away with robes and gowns and all those nursery doll dresses – men should put away childish things. A cross on the back is the sign of a devil in the heart. If you want to dress as Rome does, go to Rome and wave her banner as you do.

Priests who think that they get the respect of honest men by their fancy ornamental dresses are sadly mistaken. They say *fine feathers make fine birds* and:

> *An ape is ne'er so like an ape*
> *As when he wears a popish cape.*

Among us Dissenters, the preacher claims no priestly power, so why would we wear a special dress? Let fools wear fools' caps and fools' gowns, but men who make no claim to be fools should not put on fools' clothes. Only a very silly sheep would wear a wolf's clothing. It is a conspicuous taste that makes honest men covet the rags of thieves.

Besides, what's the good of such finery? Except a duck in galoshes, no creature looks sillier than a dissenting preacher in a gown which is no use to him. I've nearly split my sides laughing at some of them – puffed out like angry, inflated tom turkeys with their silk gowns, their bibs, and neck bands.

They are weak folks who want a man to dress like a woman before they can enjoy his sermon, and he who cannot preach without such garishness may be a man among geese, but he is a goose among men.

That said, the preacher should dress himself respectably, according to what he can afford. He should be neat, without spot or stain. Kings should not have dirty footmen waiting at their table, and those who teach godliness should practice cleanliness. I would like white neckties better if they stayed white, but dirty brown doesn't say much either way.

And may the church be delivered from a slovenly, smoking, snuff-taking, beer-drinking parson. I have met some who may have very fine manners – they just forgot to bring them. Like the Dutch captain with his anchors, they had left them at home.

This should never be the case, for, if there is a well-behaved man in the parish, it should be the minister. A worn coat is no disgrace – the poorest man can still be neat. If he is not, he ought to go back to being a student before he stands up to teach.

You cannot judge a horse by his harness, but it seems to me that a preacher's dress ought to be modest, respectable, and unremarkable – neither too showy nor too shabby. This little bit of my mind is meant to warn you youngsters who have just started in the ministry. If any of you get upset over it, I remind you that sore horses cannot bear to be brushed, and *if the cap fits, wear it.*

A preacher's dress ought to be modest, respectable, and unremarkable.

Some will say that John Ploughman should stick to mending his own smock and leave the parsons alone, but I presume to look around me and speak my mind. A cat may look at a king, and a fool may give good advice to a wise man. If I speak too plainly, please remember that an old dog cannot change his bark, and he who has habitually ploughed a straight furrow is bound to speak in the same straightforward manner.

On Good Nature and Firmness

"Long before they know whether it is a thief in the farmyard or the old mare running loose, they throw up the window and fire off the guns." – Page 27

Do not be all sugar, or the world will suck you down; but do not be all vinegar either, or the world will spit you out. There is a balance in all things

– only blockheads go to extremes. We don't need to be all rock or all sand, all iron or all wax. There is no sense in wagging your tail at everyone like a silly lapdog nor any virtue in flying at everyone like a surly mastiff.

Black and white make up the world, and so you will have to deal with all sorts of people. Some are as easy as an old shoe – and worth about as much – while others catch fire at the smallest spark and are as dangerous as gunpowder. It's a nuisance to have someone stomping around the farm like a bear with a sore head – sour, sharp, surly, and snapping at everyone. Yet, for all that, there may be some good points about the man. But poor soft Tommy, who bends like a willow and is as green as grass is nobody's prize and everybody's scorn. A man must have a backbone, or he'll never hold his head up – but that backbone needs to bend, or he will bruise his forehead on every beam.

There is a time to do as others wish and a time to refuse. If we make ourselves asses, we can expect to be ridden. But, if we want to be respected, we must be our own masters and not let others saddle us as they think fit. If we try to please everybody, we will be like a toad under a harrow – never at rest. And if we are always at everyone's beck and call, no one will thank us because we will soon do more harm than good. He who makes himself a sheep will find that the wolves are not all dead. He who lies on the ground must expect to be walked on. If you are a mouse, the cats will eat you. If you let people put a calf on your shoulders, they will soon throw on the cow. We are to please our neighbor for his good and for edification – but that is a different matter entirely.

There are sly old foxes whose mouths are always watering for naïve young geese, and if they can trick them into doing what they want, they will soon profit off of them. Your friends will call you a fine fellow if you let them use you, but they will overburden you with obligations, and you will have to get out of your mess alone because your old friends already got what they wanted out of you. They'll say, "Goodbye basket. I've carried all my apples," or they will give you their good wishes and nothing more. You will learn the hard way that fine words won't feed a cat, butter your bread, or fill your pockets. Those who praise you the loudest either need something from you or they mean to cheat you. When they have sucked the orange, they will throw the peel away.

Look before you leap, or your friend's advice might do you more harm than an enemy's slander.

So be wise. Look before you leap, or your friend's advice might do you more harm than an enemy's slander. *The simple believes every word, but the prudent considers well his steps* (Proverbs 14:15). Go as far with your friend as your conscience will allow, but part company when the shoe of conscience begins to pinch your foot. Start with your friend as you mean to go on, and let him know very early that you are not made of putty – you have a mind and judgment of your own, and you mean to use them. Pull back the moment you find you are off the road and take the nearest way back at once to avoid being dragged into the ditch with your friend. It's better to lose your friend than to lose your character and risk your soul.

Never be ashamed to walk down Turnagain Lane. Let them call you a turncoat when you turn from bad paths – it is better to turn in time than to burn in eternity. Do not throw yourself away to please somebody. The cost is too high. Put your foot down where you mean to stand, and don't let anyone move you off it. Learn to say, "No," and it will be of more use to you than to be able to read Latin.

A friend to everybody is often a friend to nobody. Or worse, he robs his family to help strangers and becomes brother to a beggar. There's a kind of wisdom in generosity, as in everything else, and some folks need to go to school to learn it. A kindhearted man might end up being cruel to his own children by taking their food to give to those who call him generous but laugh at his foolishness. He who lends his money often loses both his gold and his friend, and he who is surety is never sure. Take John Ploughman's advice: never be security for more than you can afford to lose. Remember, the Word of God says, *He who is surety for a stranger will suffer, but one who hates being surety is secure* (Proverbs 11:15).

When someone hurts us, we are bound as Christians to bear it without malice, but we do not need to pretend we don't feel it. That would only encourage our enemies to kick us again. If you get cheated twice by the same man, half the blame is yours. And in other matters, if we do not claim our rights, it is our fault if we do not get them. Paul was willing to suffer for his Master's sake, but he did not forget to tell the magistrates that he was a Roman. And when they tried to hush things up and sneak him out of prison, he said, *"No indeed! Let them come themselves and get us out"* (Acts 16:37). A Christian is the gentlest of men – but he is still a man.

Many people don't need to be told this, for they are up in arms at the first sign of offense. Long before they know whether it is a thief in the farmyard or the old mare running loose, they throw up the window and fire off the guns. These are dangerous neighbors; you'll find more comfort sitting on a bull's forehead than in their neighborhood. Wise Solomon told us: *Make no friendship with an angry man, and with a furious man do not go* (Proverbs 22:24). *He who is slow to wrath has great understanding, but he who is impulsive exalts folly* (Proverbs 14:29). *Do you see a man hasty in his words? There is more hope for a fool than for him* (Proverbs 29:20).

In my day, I've met some stubborn men who could not be changed by either sense or reason. A fellow in our village keeps a bulldog, and he tells me that once the creature sinks its teeth into something, he never lets go – not unless you cut his head right off. That's the kind of stubborn man that has bothered me and almost driven me crazy. It would be easier to argue a pitchfork into a threshing machine or persuade a chunk of brick to turn into marble than to get the fellow to hear common sense.

Scrubbing spots off of leopards is nothing at all compared with trying to lead a downright obstinate man. Right or wrong, you might as easily make a hill walk to London as convince him to change his mind when it is made up. When a man is right, this sticking to his text is a great thing – our minister says it is the stuff that martyrs are made of. But when an ignorant, wrongheaded fellow gets this hard grit into him, he makes martyrs of those who have to put up with him.

Old Master Pighead swore he would drive a nail into an oak board with his bare fist – and smashed his hand for life. He could not sell his corn at the price he wanted, so he let the rats eat it up. You cannot ride by his fields without noticing his obstinacy, for he vows, "He won't have none of these 'ere new-fangled notions," so he ends up with the worst crops in the parish. Worst of all, when his daughter joined the Methodists, in a towering rage, he threw her out of the house. And even though I believe he is sorry for doing it, he will not yield an inch. He is sticking by it and refusing to speak to her as long as he lives – even as she is wasting away in sorrow. Rash vows are much better broken than kept. He who never changes, never improves. He who never yields, never conquers.

With children, you must mix gentleness with firmness. They must not always have their own way, but they must not always be opposed either. Give to a pig when it grunts and to a child when it cries, and you will have a fine, fat pig and a spoiled child. A man learning trumpet and a pampered child are two neighbors I'd rather not have, but unless we are careful, our children will be a nuisance to others and a torment to ourselves.

Say what you mean and stick to it.

The rod and rebuke give wisdom, but a child left to himself brings shame to his mother (Proverbs 29:15). If we never get headaches from correcting our little children, we will have plenty of heartaches when they grow up.

Be honest and consistent. Say what you mean and stick to it – let your yes be yes and your no be no. Never promise a child and then fail to perform, whether you promise him a treat or a punishment. Disobedient children are unhappy children; for their own sakes, make them mind you. Once you yield your authority, you will rarely get it back. We must not provoke our children to anger (Ephesians 6:4) lest they become discouraged, but if we rule our household in the fear of the Lord, God will bless it.

Since John Ploughman has taken to writing, he has had many chances to show his firmness – and his gentleness too – for he has received bushels of advice. He's grateful, of course, as the squire's lady says – so grateful that he does not mind either returning the advice or giving some of his own instead. He knows it is so kind of so many people to tell him so many different ways to avoid looking stupid. He'll glean all the good that he can from the stubble, and while sticking to his own style, he will touch himself up a bit if he can. Perhaps if the minister will lend him Cowper or Milton, he may even stick a sprig of poetry in next time. But he makes no promises, for the harvest is here, and reaping leaves no time for rhyming.

The worst of it is, the kind friends who are correcting John contradict one another. One says it is very poorly done and obviously in an assumed name because the style is not rough enough for a ploughman. Another person says the matter is handled well, but the expressions are so coarse, he can't believe it gets printed.

John will give all the advice the attention it deserves. As some of the mice have been bold enough to make a nest in the cat's ear, he means to get after them and write a piece on free advice – those givers may end up with a flea in their ear in return for the advice they have given John.

On Patience

"Blow the wind never so fast, it will fall still at last." – Page 34

Patience is better than wisdom: an ounce of patience is worth a pound of brains. Everyone praises it, but few practice it. It's a medicine good for all diseases – so every old woman recommends it – but not every garden grows the herbs to make it with.

When your flesh and bones are full of aches and pains, it is as natural for us to murmur as it is for a horse to shake his head when the flies tease him or a wheel to rattle when a spoke is loose – but if nature is what rules Christians, what is the point of being one? If a soldier fights no better than a farm boy, he'd better hand in his red coat. We expect more fruit from an apple tree than from a thorn, and rightly so. The followers of a patient Savior should be patient themselves. *Grin and bear it* is the old-fashioned advice, but *sing and bear it* is even better.

After all, we deserve a lot worse than we get – the Lord's whip rarely cracks, considering what bad cattle we are. And when it does smart a little, it is soon over. Pain in the past is pleasure, and we gained experience by it. We ought not to be afraid of going down into Egypt when we know we will come out of it with jewels of silver and gold.

Impatient people water their miseries and dig up their blessings. Sorrows are visitors that come without invitation, but complaining minds send a wagon to bring their troubles home in. Many people are born crying, live complaining, and die disappointed. They chew the bitter pill, which they would not even know was bitter if they had the sense to swallow it whole in a cup of patience and water. They think every other man's burden is light and their own feathers to be heavy as lead. In their opinion, they have nothing good. No one's toes are so often stomped on by the black ox as theirs, the snow falls thickest near their door, and the hail rattles hardest on their windows. Yet, if the truth were known, it is their fancy rather than their fate that makes things go so hard with them.

Many would be well off if they just thought themselves so. A little sprig of contentment put into the poorest pot of soup will make it taste as rich as the Lord Mayor's food. John Ploughman grows the plant in his garden, but the recent hard winter nipped it terribly, so he doesn't have enough to hand it out

If you have modest means, let your wants be modest too.

to others. They had better follow Matthew 25:9, which says: *Go rather to those who sell, and buy for yourselves.* Grace is a good soil to grow it in, but it needs watering from the fountain of mercy.

It's not always pleasant to be poor, but worse things happen at sea. Small shoes are apt to pinch, but not if you have a small foot. If you have modest means, let your wants be modest too. There's no shame in being poor – but plenty in being discontented with it.

In some ways, the poor are better off than the rich: if a poor man has to seek meat for his appetite, he is more likely to get what he is after than the rich man who seeks an appetite for his meat. A poor man's table does not take long to spread, and his work and hunger means he doesn't need sauce to stir up his appetite. The best doctors are Dr. Diet, Dr. Quiet, and Dr. Merryman, and many a godly ploughman has all three attending to him.

Plenty spoils the appetite, but hunger finds no fault with the cook. Hard work brings health, and an ounce of health is worth a sack of diamonds. It is not how much we have, but how much we enjoy, that makes happiness. A spoonful of sugar tastes sweeter than a cask of vinegar. It is not the quantity of our goods but the blessing of God on what we have that makes us truly rich. The parings from a sweet apple are better than the whole fruit of a crabapple. *Better is a dinner of herbs where love is, than a fatted calf with hatred* (Proverbs 15:17). *Better is a little with the fear of the* LORD, *than great treasure with trouble* (Proverbs 15:16). A little wood will heat my little oven – why should I complain that I don't own the forest?

When trouble comes, it is of no use to fly in God's face with hard thoughts about His providence. That is just kicking *against the goads* (Acts 26:14) and hurting your feet. The trees bend with the wind, and so must we. Every time the sheep bleats, it misses a mouthful, and every time we complain, we miss a blessing. Grumbling is a bad trade – it yields no profit. But patience has a golden hand.

Trouble doesn't last forever. After rain comes shine. Black crows have wings. Every winter turns to spring, and every night breaks into morning.

> *Blow the wind never so fast,*
> *It will fall still at last.*

If one door shuts, God will open another. If the peas do not yield well, maybe the beans will. If one hen leaves her eggs, another may hatch her whole brood. There's a bright side to all things, and a good God everywhere. Even in the worst flood of trouble, somewhere there is a dry spot for contentment to stand on – and if not, it can learn to swim.

Friends, let us take to patience and water gruel, as the old folks used to tell us, and make do with what we have. If we don't, we will catch the grumbles and spread the sickness by wickedly finding fault with God. The best cure for affliction is submitting to providence. What can't be cured must be endured. If there's no bacon, thank God we have cabbages. *Must* is a hard nut to crack, but it has a sweet kernel.

All things work together for good to those who love God (Romans 8:28). Whatever falls from the skies is, sooner or later, good for the land – and whatever comes from God is worth having, even if it is a rod. Naturally, we don't like trouble any more than a mouse can fall in love with a cat, but Paul, by grace, came to *glory in tribulations* (Romans 5:3). Losses and crosses are heavy to bear, but when our hearts are right with God, even the heaviest yoke becomes light.

We must go to glory by way of Weeping Cross, and we were never promised a ride to heaven in a feather bed. Our fathers found the road to be rough, and we shouldn't be disappointed when we find it hard as well. All's well that ends well – so let's plough the hardest soil with our eyes on the harvest and sing at our work while others complain.

On Gossips

"Don't be the devil's bellows, stoking up
the fire of strife." – Page 40

In Walton church, in our county, there is an old relic – a *brank*, or "scold's bridle" – once used in years gone by to keep women's tongues from troubling their husbands and their neighbors. They did some strange things in those "good old days." Was this bridle proof of what our parson calls the "wisdom of our ancestors" or was it just plain cruelty?

It's nothing – only a woman drowning is a wicked and spiteful old saying, which, like the bridle, came from the common notion that women do a world of mischief with their tongues. Is it true or not? John Ploughman will let others decide that, for he admits that he is not great at keeping a secret himself and enjoys a bit of a chat as much as the next man. But he does not care for cracking people's characters and hates the slander that some people find so sweet.

John puts the question to wiser men than himself: Are women much worse than men in this matter? Some say *silence is a fine jewel for a woman but one not often worn.* Is it true that a woman only conceals what she does not know? Are women's tongues, like lambs' tails, always wagging? They say *a fox is all tail and a woman all tongue.* Is it so? Was that old prayer a fair one – *From big guns and women's tongues deliver us?*

John cannot be a fair judge because he has a good, quiet wife, whose voice is so sweet that he never tires of hearing it. But he does suspect that some other women would rather preach than pray and would not need strong tea to set their tongues going. But fair is fair, and what is sauce for the goose is sauce for the gander – and some men are just as fond of babbling as any woman.

It's a pity that there is not a tax on words – what an income the Queen would collect! But talking pays no toll. If lies were taxed double, the government might pay off the national debt, but who would be able to collect the money? Common fame is a common liar. Hearsay is half lies. *A tale never shrinks in the telling* – like a snowball, it grows as it rolls. Those who talk much lie much. If people only said what was true, what a peaceful world we'd live in! Silence rarely causes trouble, but talking is a plague to the whole village.

Silence is wisdom – and by that rule, wise men and wise women are scarce. Still waters are the deepest, but the shallowest brooks make the most noise. That tells us that fools aren't in short supply. An open mouth often signals an empty head. If a chest had gold or silver in it, it would not sit wide open. Talking is natural, but being quiet needs a good deal of training. A concern for truth should put a bit into every honest man's mouth and a bridle on every good woman's tongue.

If we must talk, at least let it be without slander. Let's not blister our tongues with backbiting. Slander might be sport to talebearers, but it is death to those spoken against. We can commit murder with the tongue as well as with the hand. The worst evil you can do a man is to injure his character. As the Quaker said to his dog, "I'll not beat thee nor abuse thee, but I'll give thee an ill name."

Not everyone a dog barks at is a thief, but most folks treat them as if they were. The world, for the most part, believes that where there is smoke there is fire, and what everybody says must be true. So let us be careful not to hurt people by staining their character, for it is hard to get dirt off once it is thrown on. Once a man is in people's bad books, he rarely ever gets out of them.

If you want to be sure not to speak amiss, the best way is to speak as little as possible. If all the sins of the world were divided into two bundles, half of them would be sins of the tongue. *If anyone does not stumble in word, he is a perfect man, able also to bridle the whole body* (James 3:2).

So then, gossips of both genders – give up the nasty habit of talebearing. Don't be the devil's bellows, stoking up the fire of strife. Stop setting people at odds with one another. And if you do not cut a bit off your tongues, at least season them with the salt of grace. Praise God more and criticize neighbors less.

Any goose can cackle. Any fly can find a sore. Any empty barrel can make noise. Any brier can tear a man's skin. No flies will go down your throat if you keep your mouth shut, and no evil speaking will come up.

Think much, but say little. Be quick to work and slow to speak. And above all, ask the great Lord to set a watch over your lips.

On Seizing Opportunities

"Dear me, is the train gone? My watch must have stopped in the night!" – Page 41

S ome people are never awake when the train pulls out. They crawl into the station just in time to see that everybody is gone and then sleepily say, "Dear me, is the train gone? My watch must have stopped in the night!" They always come into town the day after the fair and open their market stall after everyone has already gone home. They make their hay when the sun has stopped shining and cut their corn as soon as the fine weather ended. They cry, "Hold on!" after the gun's already been fired and lock the stable door long after the horse is gone.

They are like a cow's tail – always behind. They grab time by the heels, not by the forelock if they bother to grab it at all. They're no more useful than an old calendar. Their usefulness is gone, but unfortunately, you cannot throw them away as you would the old calendar. They are like the cross old lady who had inherited an annuity and swore she'd live long enough to get every last penny out of it. These people just won't die, even though they are of no use alive.

Take-it-easy and Livelong are first cousins, they say, and more's the pity. If they do not die until their work is done, they will live a long time, for they have not even begun to work yet. Shiftless people generally excuse their laziness by saying they are only a "little behind," but a little too late is much too late, and a miss is as good as a mile.

My neighbor Sykes got around to covering his well – after his child had drowned in it. And he was very busy hauling water out of the old farm well after every stick of the house had been burnt. One of these days, he'll be trying to make his will when he can't hold a pen, and he'll be trying to repent of his sins when his mind is already gone.

These slowpokes think that tomorrow is better than today. They live by the motto: "Never do today what you can put off until tomorrow." They are forever waiting for their ship to come in, always dreaming that things will look up soon – while weeds choke their fields and cows escape through holes in their fence. If the birds would just wait to have salt put on their tails, what a breakfast these people would take home to their families! But as it stands and things move as fast as they do, the kids at home will have to fill their mouths with empty spoons.

Those who won't plough cannot expect to eat.

"Never mind," they say, "there are better times coming – just wait." All their birds are "in the bush," and rare fat ones they are, according to them. They need to be – for they have had none in the hand yet, and the wife and children are half-starved. "Something will turn up," they say. Well, then – why don't they go and turn it up themselves? Time and tide wait for no man, but these dawdlers act as if they have unlimited time, a lifetime lease on both time and opportunity. They will find out their mistake when need finds *them* out. That will not be long with some in our village, for they are already halfway on the road to Needham. Those who won't plough cannot expect to eat. Those who waste the spring will have a lean autumn. They would not strike when the iron was hot, and now they will find the cold iron to be very hard.

> *He that will not when he may,*
> *When he will, he shall have nay.*

Time isn't tied up like a horse to a manger. It is more like the wind – and if a man wants to grind his corn by it, he must set his mill sails. He who waits to be fed with his mouth wide open will die that way. You get nothing without pain and effort except poverty and dirt.

In the old days, they used to say, *Jack gets on by his stupidity.* Jack would find it very different now, I think. But even back in the old days, Jack would not get anywhere by foolishly letting opportunities slip by him. Hares never run into the mouths of sleeping dogs. He who has time but waits for a better time will come to regret losing all of it.

Lying around crying, "God help us!" is no help at all. When I hear a man declare that the times are bad and that luck is always against him, I say to myself, "That old goose did not sit on the eggs until they all rotted, and now he wants to blame providence because they won't hatch."

I've never had much faith in luck – except to say it might help a man across a ditch if he jumps well and will put a bit of bacon into his pot if he looks after his garden and keeps a pig. Luck usually comes to those who look for it, and I believe it taps at every man's door at least once in a lifetime. But if industry doesn't answer, away it goes.

Those who have missed the last coach and let every opportunity slip by them turn to abusing providence for setting everything against them. "If I were a hatter," says one, "men would be born without heads." "If I went to the sea for water," says another, "I'd find it dried up." Every wind is foul for an unsound ship. Neither the wise nor the wealthy can help him who has long refused to help himself.

John Ploughman, in the most genteel and polite manner, sends his compliments to his friends. Now that harvest is over and the hops are picked, as promised, he intends to treat them to a bit of poetry, just to show he's trying to polish himself a little.

He asked the minister to lend him one of the poets, and he gave him the works of George Herbert – not bad, but rather tangled, like Harkaway Wood. Still, there's a good deal in the strange old verses, and every now and then one finds clusters of meaning, even if they are hard to crack. The following verse fits our subject well. John sees the reason in it, but he cannot see a rhyme. However, as it is by the great Herbert, it must be good and will do well enough to dress up John's talk, like a flower stuck in a buttonhole of his Sunday coat.

> Let your mind still be bent, still plotting where
> And when and how the business may be done.
> Slackness breeds worms; but the sure traveler,
> Though he alight sometimes, still goeth on.
> Acting and stirring spirits live alone.
> Write on the others, *Here lies such a one.*[4]

---

4 From the poem "Perirrhanterium," by George Herbert.

On Keeping One's Eyes Open

"There are plenty of baits for fishes." – Page 47

To get through this world, a man needs to stay sharp – and even sleep with one eye open. There are plenty of baits for fishes, nets for birds, and traps for men. While foxes run loose, we must not be geese.

Some people I know see more with one eye than others do with two, and some have fine eyes and still can't see a thing. All heads are not filled with sense. Some people are so cunning that they trust no one. They suspect everybody, so they live all their lives in miserable fear of their neighbors. Others are so simple that every conman takes them in and makes a quick penny off them. One man strains his eyes trying to see through a brick wall, while another finds a hole in it and looks right through it. Some work at the mouth of a furnace and never get scorched but others burn their hands just trying to warm them.

Now, you can't give another person experience – we all have to learn for ourselves – but here are a few plain tips that have served me well, and perhaps they may help others too.

Nobody looks more honest than a true fraud. When a man plasters his religion all over his shop window, you can be sure he keeps very little of it in stock. Don't choose your friends by their appearances: shiny shoes often pinch the feet. Don't be too fond of compliments. Remember, "Thank you, kitty, and thank you, kitty," was how they killed the cat.

Don't trust the one who talks the most, for mewing cats are very seldom good mousers. Never put yourself in another person's power: if you put your thumb between two grinding stones, they are very apt to bite. Don't drink without seeing what's in the cup. Don't sign anything without reading it, and make sure it doesn't mean more than it says.

Don't go to court unless you have nothing to lose

– lawyers build fine houses on the heads of fools. In business, don't wade into water where you can't see the bottom. Don't trust the label on a bag, and count the money every time. Look in the sack before you buy what is in it, for he who trades in the dark asks to be cheated.

Avoid people who do not value their own characters. Steer clear of anyone who swears – if he would blaspheme his Maker, he'll have no problem lying to or stealing from you. Beware of no man more than of yourself: we carry our worst enemies within us. When a new opinion or doctrine comes along, do not bite until you know whether it is bread or a stone, and do not trust the gingerbread just because it is covered in gold.

Beware of no man more than of yourself.

Don't shout "Hurrah!" until you are entirely out of the woods, and don't call it a fish fry until they are caught in the net and put in the pan. There's always time enough to boast – wait a little longer.

Don't throw away dirty water until you have clean. If you are scraping roads, keep at it until you find better work, for the poorest pay is better than none, and the humblest job is better than no job. Always give way to bulls and madmen, and never argue with a coal heaver or a scoundrel, for they will drag you into the dirt.

Neither trust nor contend
Nor lay wagers nor lend,
And you may depend
You'll have peace to your end.

Now, I won't say that is all that is needed for peace, but it is a good start.

Never ride a horse with bad knees. Don't deal with the trader who has once been fraudulently bankrupt. A rickety chair is a dangerous seat. Be wary of people who are over polite, and don't be too fast with those who are forward and rough. If something smells fishy, be on your guard. Set the trap as soon as you smell a rat, but be careful not to catch your own fingers.

Have little to do with a boaster for his beer is all froth. He may brag that all his goods – even his copper kettles – are gold and silver, but you will soon find that a boaster and a liar are first cousins. Don't spill all your secrets – trust in God with all your heart but measure your confidence in your friends wisely. Men are just men, and all men are frail. Do not hang a heavy weight on a thin thread.

Yet do not be overly suspicious, for suspicion is a cowardly virtue at best. Men are not angels, remember that – but they are not devils either. It's wrong to treat them as if they were.

And one thing to be sure of – never put your trust in any priest of any religion. A man doesn't become a false priest without first hardening his heart and blinding his conscience. Our government imprisons gypsies for telling fortunes, but they hand out fat paychecks to those vagabonds who deceive the people in matters more serious.

"Bad company," said the thief, walking to the gallows between the hangman and a priest. Though it was spoken in jest, it was very true speech. The ignorance of fools keeps the pot boiling for priests. May God clean this land from the plague of their presence and make men wise enough to see through their tricks.

Finally, my advice to all is to remember that real wisdom is that which proves itself wise in the end. Go seek it, friends, from the wisest teacher of all, the Lord Jesus. Trust Him, and He will never fail you. Follow His Word, and it will never mislead you. Pray in His name, and your prayers will be answered.

Remember, he who leans on man will find nothing but a broken reed, but he who builds on Christ stands on solid rock. You may follow Jesus with your eyes closed – but when others want to lead you, keep your eyes open, even if you have a dozen, and all of them as powerful as telescopes.

Thoughts About Thought

"Two heads are better than one." – Page 53

Not much of this paper can be said to be mine. Our minister, so to speak, provided the horses and steered the plough – I only cracked the whip now and then to keep folks awake. "Two heads are better than one," said the woman when she took her dog with her to market: begging his pardon, our minister is the woman in this case and the only sensible head in the whole affair. He is used to giving his people much better things than what a poor ploughman is likely to dig out of his bag, but at his request, I've sprinkled a few simple sayings into his thoughts, as he says, "by way of salt." That is a very kind way of putting it. I only hope my plain talk has not spoiled his fine writing. If he likes it, I'd be glad to tack a few more of my sayings onto his pieces in the future – and you will always be honestly told whether what you are reading is completely John Ploughman's talk or the writings of two characters rolled into one.

There are not so many hours in a year as there may be thoughts in an hour. Thoughts fly in like flocks of starlings or swarms of bees. Like the withered leaves in autumn, there are too many to count. Like links in a chain, one thought pulls in another. Man is a restless creature. His thoughts dance up and down like gnats on a summer evening. The mind, like a clock full of gears with the pendulum in full swing, moves faster than time. That's why thinking is such a serious business.

Just as many littles make a large, so many light thoughts make a great weight of sin. A grain of sand is light, but Solomon tells us that a whole heap of sand is heavy (Proverbs 27:3). When there are many children, the mother has to keep a sharp eye. We ought to keep a sharp eye on our thoughts, for if they turn into enemies, they will outnumber us and drag us down to ruin. Thoughts from heaven, like birds in spring, will fill our souls with music, but evil thoughts will sting us like vipers.

People say that thoughts are free. True, they may be toll-free, but I remember reading in the Good Book that they are not hell-free. We cannot be summoned before an earthly court for thinking, but we will have to answer for our thoughts at the Last Day. Evil thoughts are the seed of sin, the yeast that makes it rise, the tinder that catches the sparks of the devil's temptations! They are the churn where imagination is churned into purpose and plan, the nest where evil birds lay their eggs. Know this: just as fire burns brush as well as logs, God will punish thoughts of sin as well as deeds of sin.

Evil thoughts are the seed of sin.

Do not fool yourself into thinking that the Lord does not see your thoughts. He has a window straight into the secret room of your soul – a window that has no curtains. Just as we watch bees in a glass hive, so the eyes of the Lord watch us. The Bible says, *Hell and Destruction are before the LORD; so how much more the hearts of the sons of men* (Proverbs 15:11). Man is open to God. There are no secrets to heaven. What happens in the deepest corner of your heart is as public to God as the streets are to us.

But some will say that they cannot help having bad thoughts. That might be true, but the question is, *do they hate them or not?* You can't keep thieves from looking in your windows, but if you open your doors to them and welcome them in your home, you are just as guilty as they are. We cannot keep birds from flying overhead, but we can keep them from building their nests in our hair. Vain thoughts will knock at the door, but do not open the door. Sinful thoughts *rise,* but do not let them *reign.*

If a person rolls a sweet around in his mouth, it's because he likes the flavor. And when someone keeps turning over evil in his mind, it's because he loves it and is ready to act on it. Think of the devil, and he will appear. Turn your thoughts toward sin, and your hands will soon follow. Snails leave their slime behind them and so do evil thoughts. An arrow may fly through the air without a trace, but a wicked thought always leaves a trail like a serpent in the dust. Where there is a lot of traffic in the mind, there will be mud and dirt. Each wave of wicked thoughts adds more muck to the shore of life.

Once you indulge a vile imagination, it gets the key of our minds and can come back again whenever it pleases whether we want it to or not. And when it comes back, it often brings seven other spirits with it more wicked than itself. Who knows what may follow? Nurture sin in the cradle of thought, and it will grow into a giant. If you soak your mind in evil, it will flame up in sin at every opportunity like twine soaked in naphtha. This is why it is wise to watch over the thoughts and imaginations of your heart every day.

Good thoughts are blessed guests – welcome them, feed them, and seek their company often. Like rose petals in a jar, they leave a sweet fragrance in the memory. They enrich the soul like a crop that enriches the soil. As the hen broods her chickens under her wings, so should we cherish all holy thoughts. Like the poor man's ewe lamb that ate from his plate and slept in his arms, so should we treasure thoughts and meditation that draw us to God. Holy thoughts breed holy words and holy actions, and they are hopeful signs of a renewed heart. Who wouldn't want that?

To keep chaff out of a bushel, fill it full of wheat. In the same way, to keep out vain thoughts, keep your mind stored with good things. These are easy to find, and you should never be without them. May we all be able to say with David, *"In the multitude of my anxieties within me, Your comforts delight my soul"* (Psalm 94:19).

Faults

"Rotten wood will crack, and cracked
pots will leak." – Page 61

Anyone who brags about being perfect is perfectly foolish. I have been around a bit, and I have yet to see either a perfect horse or a perfect man, and I never will until two Sundays fall on the same day. You cannot get white flour out of a coal sack, and you can't get perfection out of human nature. If you look for perfection, you might as well look for sugar in the sea.

The old saying is, *Lifeless, faultless*. Only the dead are without faults, and we should speak well of them. But the living are all tarred with the same black brush, and anyone can see it. Every head has a soft spot, and every heart has its black drop. Every rose has its thorns, and every day has its night. Even the sun shows spots, and the skies are often darkened with clouds.

There is no one so wise who still doesn't have enough folly to stock a stall at Vanity Fair. There are people who are able to hide their fool's cap, but you can still hear the fool's bells jingling on them. As all sunshine comes with shadows, so all human good is mixed up with some evil. Even poor law guardians have their failings, and parish sextons are not angels. The best wine has its dregs.

A man's faults are not written on his forehead. If they were, hats would need very wide brims. Still, as sure as eggs are eggs, everyone has some sort of fault. You never know when those sins will show themselves – hares pop out of the ditch when you least expect them. A weak-legged horse may not stumble for a mile or two, but it is in him, and the rider had better keep his reins tight. The tabby cat might not be in the milk right now, but leave the dairy door open, and you'll see she is just as bad a thief as the kitten. Flint looks cool, but hit it with steel and you'll get sparks. Everyone knows this truth, but not everyone will remember to keep his gunpowder out of the candle.

If we kept in mind that we live among imperfect

people, we would not be so upset when our friends fail us. Rotten wood will crack, and cracked pots will leak. Blessed is he who expects nothing from frail flesh and blood, for he will never be disappointed. The best of men are only men at their best, and even the best wax will melt.

> *It is a good horse that never stumbles,*
> *And a good wife that never grumbles.*

But such creatures are only found in a fool's paradise – right next to where dumplings grow on trees. In this wicked world, even the straightest timber has knots, and the cleanest wheat field has weeds. The most careful driver may still tip the cart, the cleverest cook spills a little broth, and as I know from personal experience, a very decent ploughman will now and then break the plough or make a crooked furrow.

The best of men are only men at their best.

It is foolish to throw away a tried friend because of a fault or two – you might get rid of a one-eyed nag and end up with a blind one. Since we are all full of faults, we ought to keep two bears: bear and forbear. Since we all live in glass houses, none of us should throw stones. Everybody laughs when the saucepan says to the kettle, "How black you are!"

Other people's imperfections show us our imperfections, for we are more alike than we want to admit. If there's an apple in my neighbor's eye, there is no doubt one in mine. We ought to use our neighbors as mirrors to see our own faults and fix in ourselves what we see in them.

I have no patience with people who stick their noses into everyone's home, sniffing out flaws and using magnifying glasses to hunt down the tiniest defect. Those folks had better look at home – they might find the devil closer than they think. If you want to find fault, you will – whether it is there or not. Faults are always thick where love is thin. A white cow looks black if you choose to see it that way. Sniff rose water long enough, and even it will start to smell bad.

It would be a lot more pleasant – for everyone – if fault hunters turned their dogs loose to hunt out the good in others. That kind of game would pay better, and nobody would be standing with a pitchfork to keep the hunters off his property.

As for our own faults, we'd need a big slate to list them all, but thank God, we know where to take them and how to get help with them. With all our faults, God still loves us if we are trusting in His Son. So do not be discouraged. We can still, live, learn, and be useful before we die.

The cart may creak, but it will still get home with its load and the old, weak-kneed horse still has got plenty of work left in him. There's no use in lying down and doing nothing just because we cannot do everything perfectly. Faults or no faults, the ploughing still must be done – and imperfect people must do it or there will be no harvest next year. As poor a ploughman as John may be, the angels won't do his work for him, so he is off to do it himself.

Things Not
Worth Trying

"People have told me to be bold and grab
the bull by the horns." – Page 66

There's wisdom in that old saying: *Spend not all
you have; believe not all you hear; tell not all you
know, and do not all you can.* There is so much work

we could do that it would be a pity to waste a grain of our strength. If the game is not worth the candle, drop it at once. It is a waste of time to look for milk in a gatepost, blood in a turnip, or sense in a fool.

You might as well boil a flint soft before asking a covetous man for money. Don't sue a debtor who does not have two pennies to rub together – you will only be throwing good money after bad, like losing your ferret without catching a rabbit. It makes no sense to offer a mirror to a blind man: if a man is so proud that he will not see his faults, he will only get angry when you point them out. There is no use holding a lantern for a mole or talking of heaven to a man whose god is his money.

There's a time for everything, and it is a silly thing to preach to a man while he is drunk – it is casting pearls before swine. Get him sober first and then speak sense to him. If you lecture him while he is drunk, you look drunk yourself.

Don't set a cat to drive a coach and do not put people into roles they're not suited for. You can't make apples from plums, and you can't make big minds out of small ones by giving them a title or an office. It's no good turning a monkey into a minister or a maid into a mistress before she's ready. Many preachers would have made better tailors or shoemakers. When God means a creature to fly, He gives it wings, and when He intends men to preach, He gives them abilities.

It is a pity to push a man into the war if he cannot fight. Do not help a man up a ladder if he's only going to fall off and break his neck. You cannot make a silk purse out of a sow's ear, and pigs will never play well on the flute, no matter how long you teach them.

There's no wisdom in aiming at impossibilities – it is a waste of powder to fire at the man in the moon. Trying to make planks out of sawdust makes more sense than some of the schemes some of my London friends fall for – like buying shares in shady companies. They'll just as soon catch the wind in a net or carry water in a sieve. Bubbles are fine fun for little boys, but bubble companies burst and leave people broke. Even if you have money you can afford to lose, there is no reason to hand it over to crooks. If I had **Don't paint lilies or garnish the gospel.** to lose a leg, I would not ask a shark to snap it off for me. Give your money to fools sooner than let rogues wheedle you out of it.

Don't do unnecessary things. Never grease a fat sow or praise a proud man. Don't make clothes for fish or coverings for altars. Don't paint lilies or garnish the gospel. Never bind up a man's head before it is broken or comfort a conscience that feels no guilt. No one needs a candle to see the sun or proof for what everyone already believes.

Do not attempt something that will cost more than it is worth. You might sweeten a dunghill with lavender water, and a sinful man might put on a nice religious front, but in the end, it will not be worth the trouble. If our nation had any sense, it would sweep out a good many costly but useless folks – people who live off the system but give nothing in return. To pay a man a pound for earning a penny is wiser than keeping scores of bishops who meet together and talk about the best way to do nothing. If my master's old dog was half as lazy as the bishops are, he would get shot or drowned because he wouldn't be worth the price of a dog license. However, their payday is coming – sure as Christmas.

I've learned not to argue over people's tastes and opinions. You might as well argue about what you can see in a fire. It makes as much sense to plough the air as it does to try to convince a man who's made up his mind about something that doesn't really matter. And never try to end a quarrel by getting angry – it is like pouring oil on a fire to put it out.

Some people like trouble. I don't envy them. I'd rather walk ten miles to get out of a dispute than half a mile to get into one. People have told me to be bold and grab the bull by the horns, but if you ask me, that is only fun if you are already so cracked that an ugly poke with a horn would not damage your skull. Solomon said, *Stop contention before a quarrel starts* (Proverbs 17:14), which is another way of saying *quit while you are ahead.*

When you see a mad dog, don't argue with him unless you are sure of your logic. Get out of his way. If anybody calls you a coward for avoiding trouble, there is no need to call him a fool – everyone knows that. Meddling in quarrels never pays. Don't stir up hornets' nests, and don't pull down old houses over your head. Meddlers will hurt their own characters; if you scrub other people's pigs, you will soon need scrubbing yourself.

There is nothing more foolish than interfering between a husband and his wife. They will stop fight-ing each other and turn on you – and it will serve you right. If you stick your spoon into someone else's soup and get scalded, who is to blame but yourself?

Here's one more bit of advice: don't waste your breath trying to change a strong-minded woman. As the rhyme goes:

If she will, she will – you can depend on't:
If she won't, she won't – and there's an end on't.

I'll close with a clipping I found in an American newspaper:

"Dip the Mississippi dry with a teaspoon; twist your heel into the toe of your boot; send up fishing hooks with balloons and fish for stars; ride a gossamer thread to chase a comet; when the rain is coming down like Niagara Falls, remember where you left your umbrella; choke a flea with a piece of brick – in short, prove that the impossible is possible – but never try to coax a woman into saying yes when she's made up her mind to say no."

Debt

"The poor debtor was set free, like a bird
let out of a cage." – Page 71

When I was just a small boy, still wearing pin-afores and attending a little dame school, I happened to lose my slate pencil but had no money to buy another one with. I did not dare ask at home.

Because I lost my pencils so often, I was afraid of being scolded for being careless. So what was young John to do? There was a little shop nearby where old Mrs. Dearson sold nuts, cakes, tops, and balls. Sometimes I had seen boys and girls get trusted by the old lady. I argued with myself that Christmas was coming, and surely someone would give me a penny – maybe even a whole silver sixpence! So I decided to go into debt for a pencil and be sure to pay at Christmas.

I did not feel easy about it, but I mustered up the courage and went into the shop. One farthing was the amount, and as I had never owed anything before and my credit was good, the pencil was handed over by the kind woman, and *I was in debt*. It didn't feel right. I felt as if I had done something wrong, but I didn't know how soon I would pay for it. How my father came to hear of this little stroke of business I never knew, but some little bird or other whistled it to him, and he came down on me hard. God bless him for it. He was a sensible man, not a child-spoiler. He did not intend to bring up his children to speculate and play at what big rogues call financing; therefore, he knocked my getting into debt on the head at once, and there was no mistaking it. He gave me a very powerful lecture about getting into debt – how it was like stealing, how it ruins lives, and how a boy who would owe a farthing might one day owe a hundred pounds and end up in prison, shaming his family.

It was quite a lecture. I can still hear it echoing in my ears. Then he marched me off to the shop like a deserter marched into the barracks. I cried bitterly all the way down the street, and felt dreadfully ashamed, because I thought everybody knew I was in debt. The farthing was paid amid many solemn warnings, and the poor debtor was set free, like a bird let out of a cage. How sweet it felt to be out of debt! My little heart vowed that nothing would ever tempt me into debt again! It was a fine lesson, and I have never forgotten it. If every child were taught the same lesson when they are young, it would be as good as a fortune to them and save them mountains of misery in years to come. God bless my father, and may England have many more like him, for our country is rotting with villainy, debt, scams, and schemes.

Debt is degrading.

Ever since that day, I have hated debt like Martin Luther hated the pope. If I say some fierce things about it, it is because I feel fiercely about it. To keep debt, dirt, and the devil out of my cottage has been my greatest wish ever since I set up housekeeping. The devil sometimes has gotten in by the door or the window, for the old serpent will wriggle through the smallest crack, but thanks to a good wife, hard work, honesty, and scrub brushes, the other two have not crossed the threshold.

Debt is degrading. If I owed a man a penny, I would walk twenty miles in the dead of winter to pay him rather than carry that burden. I would be more comfortable with peas in my shoes, a hedgehog in my bed, or a snake up my back than with unpaid bills hanging over my head. Poverty is hard, but debt is horrible. A man might as well have a smoky house and a scolding wife, which are said to be the two worst evils of our life. You can be poor but still respectable – John Ploughman and his wife hope they are and will be. But a man in debt will be talked about by the neighbors and will even lose his self-respect.

Some people seem to enjoy owing money. Not me. I'd rather be a cat stuck in a chimney over a fire, a fox with the hounds at my heels, a hedgehog on a pitchfork, or a mouse under an owl's claw. An honest man thinks a wallet full of other people's money is worse than an empty one. He cannot bear to eat food that belongs to others, wear other people's clothes or shoes. He won't rest easy while his wife is wearing bonnets and flannels that still belong to the people who made them. Like the jackdaw in peacock feathers, debtors will soon be stripped bare, and the poverty that follows will be bitter because it carries shame.

Too many folks live beyond their means. They can barely afford to keep a rabbit, but they must drive a pony and chaise. Extravagance is the common disease of the times, and many professing Christians have caught it, to their shame and sorrow. Good, plain gowns are not good enough anymore; girls must have silks and satins. The bill that comes from the dressmaker is as long and dreary as a winter's night. All that show and style and finery keeps a family poor and the father's nose to the grindstone.

Frogs try to look as big as bulls and burst themselves. Men burn the candle at both ends, and then say they are very unfortunate – why don't they put the saddle on the right horse and say they are extravagant? Economy is half the battle in life; it is not so hard to earn money as to spend it well. Hundreds would never have known *want* if they had not first known *waste*. If all poor men's wives knew how to cook, how far a little might go!

Our minister says the French and the Germans beat us hollow in nice but inexpensive cooking. I wish they would send missionaries over to convert our gossiping women into good managers. This is a French fashion that would be a great deal more useful than those fine pictures in Mrs. Frippery's window, with ladies decked out in a new style every month.

Some people are too proud to eat what their fathers were thankful to see on the table, so they please their palates with expensive food but end up in the poorhouse, expecting everyone to pity them. They turned up their noses at bread and butter – now they are eating raw turnips they stole from someone's field. Those who live like fighting cocks at someone else's expense will get their combs cut or perhaps get roasted for it one of these days. If you have a great surplus of peas, you may put more in the soup, but everyone should eat and live according to the money he makes.

He is both a fool and a crook who earns a shilling and spends a pound that does not belong to him. *Cut your coat according to your cloth* is sound advice, but cutting it from someone else's cloth by running into debt is plain theft. If I wanted to be a rogue, I would be a petty lawyer, a priest, open a loan office, or pick pockets, but I wouldn't stoop to the dirty business of getting into debt without the expectation of being able to pay.

Debtors almost always end up as liars too. They

promise to pay when they know they cannot, then make excuses and promise again. They lie as fast as a horse can trot. As the saying goes:

You have debts, and make debts still,
If you've not lied, lie you will.

If owing leads to lying, who can say that it is not an evil thing? Of course, there are exceptions. I am not talking about the honest man who is brought down by sickness or unexpected heavy losses, but in general, you will find debt to be a great, stinking, dismal swamp. Happy is the man who escapes it after tumbling in: happier still is the one who has been, by God's goodness, kept out of the mire altogether.

Without debt, without care; out of debt, out of danger.

Once you ask the devil to dinner, it is hard to get him out of the house. It's better to have nothing to do with him. Where a hen has laid one egg, she is likely to lay another, and once a man gets in debt, he is likely to get into it again. It is better to keep clear of it from the first. He who gets in for a penny will soon be in for a pound. If you never owe a farthing, you will never owe a guinea.

If you want to sleep soundly, buy the bed of a man who is in debt – it must be the softest bed in the world or he never could have rested so easy on it. An honest man who cares for his honor would rather go hungry than feast on borrowed money and would choke on dust before he would run up a tab in the pub.

Bills must stick pins and needles into a fellow's soul!

A pig on credit always grunts. Without debt, without care; out of debt, out of danger. But owing and borrowing are bramble bushes full of thorns. If I borrow a spade from my neighbor, I never feel safe because I am afraid I will break it. I can never dig as I do with my own. But if I had bought that spade on credit and knew I could not pay for it, I think I would dig my own grave out of shame.

Scripture says, *Owe no one anything* (Romans 13:8). That doesn't mean "pay your debts" – it means "don't have any." Those who willfully break this law ought to be turned out of the church.

The laws of our country shamefully encourage people to use credit. Nobody need be a thief now – you can just open a shop, fail in business, and you will come out richer. The saying is, *He who never fails will never grow rich*, and I know men who have failed five or six times, yet still think they are on the road to heaven. Heaven? What would those scoundrels do if they got there? They are more likely to go where they will never come out until they have paid the last farthing. But people say, "How generous they are!" Yes, with other people's money. I hate to see a man steal a goose and then give the church the giblets. Piety by all means, but pay your way as part of it. Honesty first, and then generosity.

But how often religion is a cloak for deception! There's Mrs. Scamp, dressed as fine as a peacock. The girls are at boarding school, learning French and the piano; the boys lie around and are treated like royalty. G. B. Scamp, Esq., drives a fast-trotting mare and takes the chair at public meetings, while his poor creditors cannot get more than enough to barely live on. It is shameful and more than I can take to see how genteel swindling is winked at by many in this country. I'd tear off their white waistcoats, kid gloves, and patent leather boots and make them work their debt off in prison. Gentlemen or not, I'd let them see that big rogues could dance grinding grain to the same tune as little ones. If I were a member of Parliament or a prime minister, I'd make the land too hot to hold for such rascals. I don't have that power, but I can at least write against the fellows and let off the steam of my wrath in that way.

My motto is, "Pay as you go." Keep short accounts. Know what you are worth by paying what you owe. It's better to go to bed hungry than to wake up in debt.

Sins and debts are always more than you think. Little by little a man gets in over his head and ears. It is the petty expenses that empty the purse. Money is round and rolls away easily. Tom Thriftless buys what he doesn't need because it is a great bargain, and soon he is made to sell what he does need. He cannot say "No" to his friend who wants him to be security. He throws fancy parties, takes many vacations, dresses his wife in frills, and never looks after his servants and still is surprised when the bills come due and that the creditors are so loud.

He has sowed his money in the field of thoughtlessness, and now he wonders why he has to reap the harvest of poverty. He hopes for something to help him out of difficulty, and so he schemes himself into more trouble, forgetting that hope and expectation are a fool's income. Being hard up, he goes to the market with empty pockets and buys at whatever prices tradesmen charge him, so he pays more than double and gets deeper into the mire. This leads him to scheming and trying little tricks, for it is hard for an empty sack to stand upright. This is not the answer because schemes are like spiders' webs – fit only for catching flies and easily swept away. A failing business propped up with tricks and schemes will be as successful as mending your shoes with paper or fixing a broken window with ice.

And when the schemer is found out, he is like a dog in church, whom everyone kicks at or like a barrel of powder, which nobody wants for a neighbor.

They say poverty is a sixth sense, and it needs to be, for many debtors seem to have lost the other five or were born without common sense. They appear to believe that not only is it okay to make debts, but you can also pay them by borrowing. Trying to pay Peter with what you borrowed from Paul is nonsense. You are only putting one foot in the mud to pull the other out. It is hard to shave an egg or pull hairs out of a bald head, but they are both easier than paying debts out of an empty pocket. Samson was a strong man, but he could not pay debts without money, and only fools think they can do it by scheming.

Borrowing money from a loan society or credit union is like a drowning man grabbing at razors; when people lend money, they generally pluck the geese as long as they have any feathers. If you want to get out of debt, you must cut back what you spend and save what you make. You can't spend your penny and pay debts with it too. Short the kitchen if the purse is bare.

Don't believe in any way of wiping out debts except by paying hard cash. Promises make debts, and debts make promises, but promises never pay debts. Promising is one thing, and performing is quite another. A good man's word should be as binding as an oath, and he should never promise to pay unless he can keep it. Those who stave off payment by false promises deserve no mercy. It is all very well to say, "I'm very sorry," but:

> *A hundred years of regret*
> *Pay not a farthing of debt.*

Now I might as well have given this advice to the chickens as to those who have already got into the habit of spending what is not their own. Advice to such people goes in one ear and out the other, but those who won't listen will have to feel, and those who refuse cheap advice will have to buy expensive change.

But to you young people beginning life, a word may save you a world of trouble. So here is John Ploughman's short sermon in three short points:

- Always live a little below your means.

- Never get into debt.

- Remember:

> *He who goes a borrowing*
> *Goes a sorrowing.*

Home

Merry times in Ploughman's Cottage.

The word *home* always sounds like poetry to me. It rings like wedding bells – only softer and sweeter – and it chimes deeper into my heart. Whether it means a thatched cottage or a manor house, home is home, be it ever so humble, and there's no place on earth quite like it. May the houseleek keep growing on the roof and let the moss flourish on the old thatch. I love the way the sparrows chirp and the swallows twitter around the place that is my rest and joy.

Every bird loves its own nest. The owl thinks the ruins are the fairest spot under the moon, and the fox is satisfied with his cozy hole in the hill. When my master's horse knows that he is heading home, he needs no whip – he goes full steam! I feel just the same: the road home is the best road in the country. I'd rather see the smoke coming from my own chimney than the fire on another man's hearth. There's something so beautiful about the way it curls up among the trees.

Every bird loves its own nest.

Cold potatoes on my own table taste better than roast beef at my neighbor's. The honeysuckle at my own door is the sweetest I have ever smelled. Friends try to make you feel welcome, but it still is not home. That is why they say, *Make yourself at home* – because everyone knows there is nothing like feeling at ease in your own place.

> *East or west,*
> *Home is best.*

At home, you are at home, and what more do you want? You don't have to watch your appetite or worry about damp sheets. You are safe in your own castle, like a king in his palace. In his own home, a man feels like somebody and is not afraid of being thought proud for thinking so. Every rooster may crow on his own dunghill, and even a little dog is a lion when he's at home. A chimney sweep is the master of the house inside his own door.

There is no need to guard every word for fear someone is listening to hurt you, no need to lock up your heart. Once the door is closed, it's Liberty Hall, and no one is watching or judging. There is a glorious view from the top of Leith Hill and other lovely spots in Surrey – Hindhead, Martha's Chapel, and Box Hill – but I can show you something even better. It's my own little cottage with the kettle singing on the hob like an unfallen black angel, the cat sleeping in front of the fire, my wife in her chair mending stockings, and the children playing around the room like little lambs.

You may not believe it, but our children are the finest you will ever see – plumper and prettier than anyone else's. And they don't tire us out like other people's children do. Why, my wife would be worn out in half the time if she were watching the neighbor's baby, but her own children don't seem to tire her at all. I reckon it is because they were born at home. Just like everything else, our lane is the loveliest in twenty miles because it leads to our home. My garden is a perfect paradise, for no other reason than that it belongs to the old house at home.

I can't for the life of me understand why so many working men spend their evenings at the pub when their own fireside would be so much better and cheaper too. There they sit, hour after hour, wasting their wages and their time, forgetting the dear good souls at home who are half starved for both affection and food. Their money goes into the pub owner's till when it ought to make their wives and children comfortable. As for the beer they get, it is just fools' milk, brewed to drown what little sense they've got left.

Such fellows ought to be horsewhipped, and the folks who encourage them and who profit off their bad habits deserve a taste of the whip too. Beer shops are the curse of this country – no good ever comes from them, and no one can fully tell the harm they do. The pubs were bad enough, but the beer shops are a pest. I wish the man who made the law to open them had to feed and house all the families that they have brought to ruin.

Beer shops are the enemies of home, and the sooner their licenses are taken away, the better. Poor men don't need such places and neither do the rich. They are all worse and no better, like Tom Norton's wife. Anything that hurts the home is a curse and ought to be hunted down like vermin in the hedgerows.

A husband should work to make his home happy and holy. The bird that fouls its own nest is sick, and a man who makes his home miserable is bad. Our homes should be like little churches, marked with *Holiness to the Lord* over the door. It should never feel like a prison where there are plenty of rules and order but little love and pleasure.

Marriage is not all sugar, but grace in the heart will sweeten most of the sour. Godliness and love can make a man sing even when he is in the thorns and can help others sing along too. A husband should delight in pleasing his wife, and the wife should care deeply for her husband. A man is being kind to himself when he is kind to his wife. But when selfishness rules the home, happiness is a mere sham.

When husbands and wives are well yoked, life's load becomes lighter, but not every couple that is married is a pair – and that's a pity. In a true home, the only competition and strife is to see who can do the most to make the family happy. A home should be a *Bethel*, not a *Babel*. The husband should be the "houseband," holding things together, not grinding everyone down. Unkind and domineering husbands have no right to call themselves Christians, for they act opposite to Christ's commands.

Still, a home must be well ordered, or it will turn into a madhouse and shame the whole neighborhood. If the father drops the reins, the family coach will soon be in the ditch. A wise mixture of love and firmness is needed, but neither harshness nor softness alone will keep the home in happy order.

A house where the children do not obey is no home at all – it is more pain than pleasure. Blessed is the man who finds joy in his children, and blessed are the children who find joy in their father. Not all fathers are wise. Some spoil their children like Eli did – and they will reap what they sow. If you never correct your children, do not be surprised when they become your punishment. Solomon said, *Correct your son, and he will give you rest; yes, he will give delight to your soul* (Proverbs 29:17). I doubt that anyone today is wiser than Solomon, though some think they are.

Children must be taught while they are young – break the colt early, or it will turn wild. Some fathers are all fire and fury, flying into rages at the smallest fault. This is worse than the other, and makes home a little hell instead of a heaven. Too little wind won't turn the mill, but too much wind wrecks it. Men who strike in their anger generally miss their mark.

But when God helps a man hold the reins firmly without hurting the horses' mouths, all goes well. When home is ruled by God's Word, even angels could spend the night with us and feel right at home.

Wives should feel that home is their place and their kingdom, and its happiness depends mostly on them. A nagging wife drives her husband away by her sharp tongue. One poor fellow told his wife to "double up her whip" – meaning give your tongue a rest. It is miserable living under the lash of constant complaints.

When home is ruled by God's Word, even angels could spend the night with us and feel right at home.

When God gave to men ten measures of speech, the old joke says women ran off with nine. Sadly, there is truth in that sometimes. A dirty, slovenly, gossiping wife is enough to drive her husband mad. If he ends up at the pub, she is often to blame.

It is a sorry life when the woman, instead of honoring her husband, is always nagging and yelling at him. It is a mercy when such women go hoarse. It is a pity that they do not have as many blisters on their tongues as they have teeth in their jaws. God save us all from wives who are angels in the streets, saints in the church, and devils at home.

I have never lived with that kind, thank God, but I deeply pity those who do.

Show me a loving husband, a worthy wife, and good children, and I'll show you a sight more beautiful than anything a pair of horses could ever carry me to in a year. Home is the finest institution. Talk about Parliament if you want, but give me a quiet little parlor. Boast about voting and the Reform Bill if you like, but I want to weed my garden and teach my children their hymns. The right to vote might be grand, but I would much rather hold the title to my cottage – if I could find the money to buy it. I don't know much about the Magna Charta, but if it means a quiet home for everybody, then three cheers for it!

It breaks my heart how the Poor Law wrecks the homes of hardworking men – it is more fit for savages than Englishmen. A Hampshire carter told me how he lost his home. His wife and eight children were all forced into the union workhouse, while he was left alone, broken and homeless. He earned nine shillings a week – not enough to live on, especially with rent. A little help – a loaf or two, a few shillings – would have kept them afloat, but the parish would not give even a penny unless they all went into the workhouse. So, with tears and heartache, the poor soul had to sell his few little bits of furniture, and now he has no home at all. He is a good, hard-working fellow and served one master for nearly twenty years.

This is very common, but it shouldn't be. Why can't the truly deserving poor receive a little help without having to surrender their homes? Why must they be forced into the union house? Home is the pillar of the British Empire, and it shouldn't be knocked to pieces by these unchristian laws. If I were an orator and could talk politics, I would speak up like a lion for the poor man's home, which, I would tell the members of Parliament, is as dear to him as their great palaces are to them – perhaps even dearer.

If I had no home, the world would feel like one big prison. Give me England for my country, Surrey for my county, and for a village give me – no, I won't tell you or you will be hunting John Ploughman up. Many of my friends have emigrated to Australia or America. Though their stone has rolled, I hope they may gather moss, for when they were at home they were like the sitting hen who gets no barley. These hard times make a man think of his wings, but I am tied to my own home, and God willing, I hope to live and die among my own people. They may do things better in France and Germany but give me old England still.

Men Who Are Down

"Where there's a carcass, the eagles gather." – Page 88

No one's life story is complete until it is over. Life is full of twists and turns, and fortune changes hands quickly. The man riding in the carriage today may be cleaning it tomorrow. Workers switch places – the one on top may soon have to take a turn in the pit. And in less than a thousand years, we will all be bald and broke anyway – who knows what could happen before then?

The thought that we ourselves might one day be begging under someone else's window should make us careful when we are throwing out our dirty water. *With the measure you use, it will be measured back to you* (Matthew 7:2), so let's treat those who fall on hard times with compassion, not cruelty.

Nothing makes me sicker of human nature than seeing the way people treat others when they fall down the ladder of fortune. "Down with him," they cry. "He always was good for nothing."

> *Down among the dead men, down, down, down,*
> *Down among the dead men – there let him lie.*

Dog won't eat dog, but men will devour each other like cannibals and boast about it too. There are thousands in this world who swoop in like vultures the minute a tradesman or a merchant gets into trouble. Where there's a carcass, the eagles gather. Instead of offering a little help, they heap on shame and cruelty, crying, "Serves him right."

The world loves to beat a man when he is already bruised. If providence strikes him, people show up with their whips. The dog is drowning, so all his friends throw buckets of water on him. The tree has fallen, and everybody runs for his hatchet. The house is on fire, and the neighbors warm themselves at the flames. The unlucky man is treated poorly. He's tumbled into the road, and they drive their carts over him. He is down, and selfishness cries, "Keep him down. There will be more room for us up here!"

It's maddening when those who knock you down kick you for not standing up! They tell you that you were a fool and you should have known better. They say you made a bad move: "Even Tom Fool can see your mistake." "He ought to have locked the stable door," they say, but no one offers to buy him a new horse. "What a pity he went so far on the ice!" That's true, but that won't save the poor fellow from drowning. When a man's coat is threadbare, it is an easy thing to pick a hole in it. Good advice is poor food for a hungry family.

> It's maddening when those who knock you down kick you for not standing up!

> *A man of words and not of deeds,*
> *Is like a garden full of weeds.*

Lend me a bit of string to tie up my broken traces and find fault with my old harness when I get home. Feed my old horse a few oats and *then* tell him to pick up his pace. It's one thing to feel for me, but if you really care, feel in your pocket, or your feelings aren't worth a fig.

Most men who go downhill meet a Judas before they get to the bottom. Those they helped in better days often forget the debt – or worse, repay it with cruelty. The young sprout runs away with the sap from the old tree. The foal feeds on his mother, then kicks her. The old saying is, *I taught you to swim, and now you'd drown me* – and it happens every day.

The dog wags his tail until he gets the bone, then he snaps and bites the hand that fed him. Eaten bread is forgotten, and the hand that gave it is despised. The candle that lit others is burnt away itself. A good deed is soon erased. *Every man for himself* is the world's golden rule, and we all know who takes the hindmost. The fox looks after his own skin and isn't going to give up his tail for a friend.

A noble spirit sides with the weak, but noble spirits are rare. They are as scarce as eagles. Magpies, hawks, and kites are common, but you may see the nobler breed only once in a lifetime. Did you ever hear a flock of crows read the burial service over a dead sheep before eating it? Well, that's how neighbors act: "Oh, what a pity! How did it happen? Oh, dear! Oh, dear!" – then each rushes in to snatch a share of the plunder.

Most people are generous to those who do not need it. Every traveler throws a stone where there is already a pile. Every cook bastes the fat pig, while the lean one gets burnt.

> *In times of prosperity, friends will be plenty;*
> *In times of adversity, not one in twenty.*

When things are going well, everyone is helpful. As long as the pot boils, friendship blooms. But flatterers do not visit cottages, and no one courts a faded rose. Everyone is related to the rich man, but even the poor man's brother does not know him. If you have a ewe and a lamb, everyone cries, "Welcome, Peter!" If the squire whispers, half the county hears him, but Widow Needy can't make herself heard through an open fence.

Men willingly pour water into a full tub and give feasts for those who are not hungry because they expect a feast in return. Have a goose and get a goose. If you have a horse of your own, you can borrow one. It is considered safe to lend barley to the one whose barn is full of wheat, but who lends or gives to the truly needy? Who, indeed, unless it is some antiquated old soul who believes in his Bible, loves his Lord, and gives, *hoping for nothing in return* (Luke 6:35)?

I have noticed certain "gentlemen" who pretend to be great friends to a falling man because there is still a bit of meat on his bones. A lawyer or moneylender will act like they want to help, then peck at him with their bills until there's nothing left. When these folks are polite and considerate, poor men need to be cautious. It's the fox greeting the hens in the coop: "Good morning to you all, my very dear friends."

Still, those who are down must not despair, for God is still alive, and He is the friend of the friendless. If no one else offers a helping hand, the Lord's hand will bring deliverance to those who trust Him. A good man may be put in the fire, but he cannot be burned. His hope may be drenched but not drowned. He gathers his courage, puts his heart into it, and climbs the steep hill. When others lie down in despair, he presses on over the rough ground.

While there's life, there's hope. So, my friend, if you've tumbled off the back of prosperity, John Ploughman tells you to not lie in the ditch. Get up and try again. Jonah went to the bottom of the sea, but he got to shore again better for the journey.

Though the bird's in the net,
It may get away yet.
Though I'm down in the dust,
In my God I will trust,
I will hope in Him still,
And submit to His will.
For He'll surely appear,
And will banish my fear.

Never forget – when a man is down, he has a grand opportunity to trust God. False faith can only float in smooth water, but true faith, like a lifeboat, is at home in storms. If our religion can't carry us through trouble, what good is it? If we only trust God when things are going our way, then we don't trust Him at all.

We trust a thief as far as we can see him, but do we dare to treat our God like that? No, no. The Lord is good; He will appear to His servants, and we will praise His name (Psalm 90:16).

"Down among the dead men." No, sir, not I.
Down among the dead men, I will not lie.
Up among the hopeful, I will ascend,
Up among the joyful, I'll sing without end.

Hope

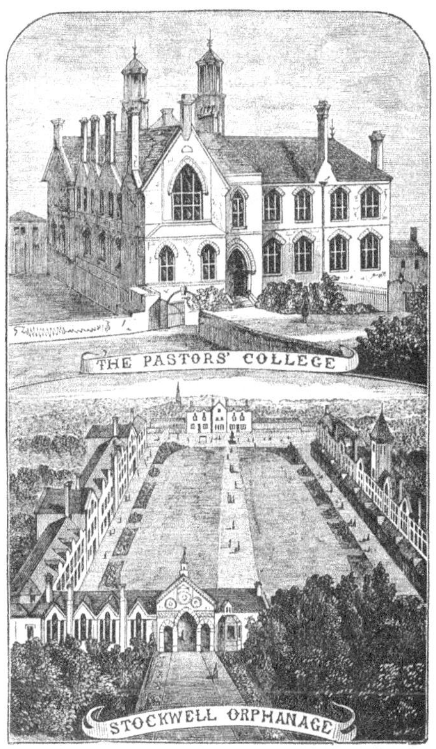

Eggs are eggs – but some are rotten. And hopes are hopes – but many of them turn out to be delusions. Hopes are like women – there is a touch of angel in every one of them, but there are two sorts. My boy Tom has been blowing out a lot of birds' eggs and stringing them together. I have been doing the same thing with hopes. Here's a few of the good, bad, and indifferent.

The optimistic man's hope pops up like a jack-in-the-box. It springs out of nowhere and has nothing to do with reason. Whenever this man looks out of the window, he sees better times coming. It may all be in his imagination, but it is more cheerful to see plum puddings in the moon than to croak at everything like a two-legged frog.

This is the kind of brother you'd want to be on the road with on a dark, stormy night, for he carries candles in his eyes and a fireside in his heart. You can keep his company if you are careful not to let him lead you into foolishness. His fault is that he counts his chickens before they are hatched and sells his herrings before they are in the net. Every little sparrow's egg is bound to turn into a thrush, if not a partridge or pheasant. He sees one swallow and declares that summer has come.

His new shop had only been open for five minutes when two neighbors came in – one for a loaf of bread on credit and the other to make change – but that was all the proof he needed to be sure he was going to make a fortune. He is certain that the squire means to give him his business because he saw him reading the name over the shop door as he rode past. He makes certainties out of maybes. But even though he is a little soft at times, there is much in him to praise, and I like one of his odd sayings, "Never say *die* till you are dead – and then it's no use, so let it alone." There are other odd people in the world besides John Ploughman.

My neighbor Shiftless is different. He's waiting for his aunt to die, but the old lady has as many lives as nine cats, and I suspect that when she does die, she will leave what little she has to the Hospital for Diseased Cats or Stray Dogs before giving it to him. Meanwhile, he's getting more and more discouraged and blames it all on the dear old lady's good health.

However, he hopes on and gets worse and worse, for while the grass grows, the horse starves. He who waits for another's death pulls at a long rope. He who hunts after legacies needs to have iron shoes. He who waits for dead men's shoes may have to go barefoot for a long time, and he who waits for his uncle's cow had better not be in a hurry to spread the butter. Living on hope makes for a slim diet. If Jack Shiftless had never had an aunt, he might have rolled up his sleeves and worked for himself, but they told him that he was born with a silver spoon in his mouth, and now he is as useful at work as a cow chasing rabbits.

He who waits for another's death pulls at a long rope.

If anybody wants to leave John Ploughman a legacy, he'd be obliged to them, but it would be best not to mention it or he might not plough as straight a furrow. Better to double it and surprise him. Still, it might do more good to leave it to the Pastors' College or the Stockwell Orphanage, for it will be well used in either case. Did you notice the drawings of these two places a page or two back? Keep them in your mind's eye.

But now we must get back to our subject. I wish people would think less about windfalls and plant more apple trees. Hopes that grow out of graves are grave mistakes, especially when they rob a man of the energy to work for himself. That sort of hope is a rope around the neck, not a lifeline.

Some people were clearly born on the first of April. They are always hoping – without sense or reason. Their ship is always about to come in. They expect to dig up a pot of gold or to hear something to their advantage. They have wind in their brains and dream while wide awake.

They might sit there a long time with their mouths open before fried ham and eggs will come flying into them, yet they really seem to believe that some stroke of luck, some windfall of golden apples, will one day set them up and make gentlemen of them. They hope to ride in their coaches, but eventually find themselves shut up in a place where the coaches won't run over them. You may whistle a long time before a goldfinch will hop onto your thumb.

Once in a while, one man in a million may stumble on a fortune, but thousands ruin themselves by idle expectations. Expect to get half of what you earn, a quarter of what is your due, and none of what you have lent, and you will be near the mark; but to look for a fortune to fall from the moon is to vigorously play the fool. A man ought to hope within the bounds of reason and the promises of the good old Book. Hope leans on an anchor, but an anchor must have something to hold by and to hold to. A hope without grounds is a tub without a bottom, a horse without a head, a goose without a body, a shoe without a sole, a knife without a blade. Who but Simple Simon would begin to build a house at the top? There must be a foundation.

Hope is folly when a man hopes for impossibilities or looks for crops without sowing seed and happiness without doing good. Hopes like that make big boasts and small roasts. They act like a jack-o'-lantern and lead men into the ditch.[5]

There's poor Will at the workhouse, who always declares that he owns a great estate, only the rightful owner keeps him out of it. He says his name is Jenyns or Jennings, and a relative of that name has left a fortune big enough to buy the Bank of England. One day, he says, he'll get his share. Meanwhile, poor Will is only served parish broth, which he finds to be an awful poor food for such a great gentleman like himself. He has promised me an odd thousand or two when he gets his fortune, and I am going to build a castle in the air with it, and ride to it on a broomstick. Like many others, he has windmills in his head and could fit his will and the list of all his belongings on his thumbnail. Ploughing the air is not half so profitable as it is easy. Anyone who hopes in this world for more than he can get by his own earnings hopes to find apricots on a crab tree.

A man who marries a vain, lazy woman and hopes to make her a good wife might as well buy a goose and expect milk. Another takes his boys to the beer shop and trusts that they will grow up sober. He might as well put his coffeepot on the fire and expect it to shine

---

5   An old Irish folk tale told of Stingy Jack, who had tricked the devil and was cursed to wander the earth with a burning coal inside a carved-out pumpkin. People believed he misled travelers, causing them to fall into hazardous situations.

like silver. People have lost their senses when they brew with bad malt and look for good beer or set a wicked example and count on raising a respectable family.

You can hope all you want, but when you send your boy up the chimney, he'll come down black. Teaching a child to lie and then hoping that he will grow up honest will be just as successful as putting a wasp in a tar barrel and hoping he makes you honey. People won't raise their children right until they are sensible themselves.

When it comes to the next world, it is a great pity how little care people take with their hopes. If a man dies drunk, somebody will say, "I hope he's in heaven." It is one thing to wish it, but something else to *hope* it.

Men turn their faces to hell and hope to get to heaven. That's like walking into the horse pond and hoping to stay dry. Hopes of heaven are serious things and should be tried and tested by the Word of God. You can no more find heaven at the end of a wicked life than you can *gather grapes from thornbushes or figs from thistles* (Matthew 7:16).

Men turn their faces to hell and hope to get to heaven.

There is only one rock to build good hopes on – and it is not Peter, as the pope says, and it is not the sacraments as the priests insist. The only true hope for man is *the Man Christ Jesus* (1 Timothy 2:5). If we believe in Him, we are saved, just as it's written: *He who believes in the Son has everlasting life* (John 3:36).

Mind you, he *has* it *now,* and it is *everlasting,* so he won't ever lose it. There John Ploughman stands, and he is not afraid of being let down. This is a firm footing and gives him a hope firm and steady, which neither life nor death can shake.

But I'll stop there, or folks will say I am trying to turn preacher and take the bread out of the parson's mouth. But please remember: Presumption is a ladder that will break the climber's neck. As you love your soul, do not climb it.

Spending

"What their fathers earned with the rake, the sons
toss away with the shovel." – Page 102

Earning money is the easy part – spending it wisely is a much bigger challenge. Anybody can dig up potatoes, but not one woman in ten can cook them well. Men do not become rich by what they get, but by what they save. Many men who have money are as short of sense as a hog is of wool. They may be over forty but still haven't reached the age of discretion. They throw away hundreds as boys throw skipping stones.

What their fathers earned with the rake, the sons toss away with the shovel. After the miser comes the prodigal. People often say of the spendthrift, "His father never helped anyone but himself, and now the son is no one's enemy but his own." The fact is, the old gentleman went to hell by the lean road, and his son has made up his mind to go there by the fat. The minute the prodigal gets his estate, it vanishes like a lump of butter in a greyhound's mouth.

Every day for him is the first of April. He'd buy an elephant if he thought it was a deal or thatch his house with pancakes. Nothing is too foolish to tickle his fancy. His money burns holes in his pocket, and he must spend it – boasting that his motto is, "Spend, and God will send." He won't wait for the sheep before shearing them – spending money before he's earned it, living on credit, dipping into his savings, killing the goose that lays the golden eggs – and then cries out shocked, "How did this happen?"

He says he means to save, but he spares no expense. He borrows at high interest from Rob'em, Cheat'em, and Sell'em-out, and when he gets cleaned out, he blames it all on the lawyers or on the bad times. Times were never good for lazy prodigals – if they were good to them, they would be bad for the rest of the world.

Why men are in such a hurry to make themselves beggars is a mystery, but between betting on horses, laziness, and risky get-rich schemes, there seems to be a daily coach to Needham every day. Ready money must be quite a curiosity to some men, but they still spend like royalty. They are gentlemen without means, which is about the same as plum puddings without plums.

> *Spending your money with many a guest,*
> *Empties the larder, the cellar, and chest.*

Add a little gambling to that fast lifestyle, and money melts like a snowball in an oven. A young gambler is just an old beggar – if he lives long enough.

> *The devil leads him by the nose,*
> *Who the dice so often throws.*

There are more asses than those with four legs. Working men can be just as foolish as fine gentlemen. Fellows who have no estate but their labor and no family arms except those they work with will still spend their meager but hard-earned wages at the beershop or on trash. **Drinking water never put a man in debt.** The minute payday comes, off they go to the Spotted Dog or the Marquis of Granby to spend their fool's money to help make the landlord fat and red-faced.

Drinking water never put a man in debt, made him sick, or left his wife a widow, but some men hardly know what it tastes like. Beer, the way it is guzzled down by some working men, is nothing better than brown ruin. Dull, droning blockheads sit on the ale bench and wash out what little sense they ever had.

I do believe that farming people are better managers of their money than Londoners are, for though they have little money, their families look nice and tidy on Sundays. True, the rent isn't as bad in a village as in the town, and there's usually a small garden out back, but those Londoners earn a lot of money and can buy cheaper goods than the poor countryman can. I think it is very good management that keeps a family going on ten shillings a week in the country and bad management that can't make ends meet on twenty-five in London.

Some families are as merry as mice in malt on very small wages, and others are as wretched as rats in a trap on twice the income. Those who wear the shoes know where they pinch, but wise spending makes ninepence go further than a shilling. Some make soup out of a stone, and others can't get nourishment out of gravy beef.

Many people shop with as much sense as Samson had in both his shoulders. They do not know how to spend wisely. Shoppers ought to have a hundred eyes, but some don't even have one – and they keep it closed! People say that if fools didn't go to market, bad goods would never be sold. They never get a penny's worth for their penny. Often they are on the hunt for cheap things and forget that the cheapest things often cost the most in the long run. You cannot get a good shilling's worth from a bad product. If someone is selling five eggs for a penny, chances are four are rotten.

Poor men often buy in tiny quantities and pay for it. When you buy by the penny's worth, you are supporting your household – and someone else's. Why not buy a couple weeks' supply at once and get it cheaper? *Store is no sore.*

Some people are stingy in the wrong places and wreck the ship for a half penny's worth of tar. Others pay attention to small savings but forget greater things. They are penny wise and pound foolish. Some buy things they don't need because they are great bargains. Let me tell you – anything you don't need is expensive, even if it is cheap.

Fancy clothes are a money pit for poor people. What business does John Ploughman and other hardworking laborers have with silks and satins? It's like a blacksmith wearing a white silk apron. I hate seeing servant girls and workingmen's daughters dressed like they are trying to pass for high society. Everyone knows a tadpole from a fish, and no one mistakes a poppy for a rose.

Give me a woman in a neat, clean, sensible dress, and she will outshine all the flashy types any day. If a girl has a few shillings to spare, she should buy some good flannel for the winter before she is tempted with bright looking but useless finery. Buy what suits you, and if others don't like how it looks, they can shut their eyes. All women are good – either for something or for nothing – and their dress will generally tell you which.

Of course, we all feel that the money slips away too fast – but money is made to circulate, and there's no use hoarding it. It is bad when money runs off like a lazy servant, but it would be worse to have it stay with us and become our master. We should try, as our minister says, to "find the golden mean" – neither be stingy or extravagant.

The man who spends best is the one with the best wife. A man may earn the money, but a wise woman knows how to keep it. *The wise woman builds her house, but the foolish pulls it down with her hands* (Proverbs 14:1). According to Solomon, the wife is the real builder or the one who pulls it down.

A man won't prosper until his wife lets him. A thrifty housewife is better than a great income. A good wife and good health are a man's best wealth.

Bless their hearts, what would we do without them? They say women always want their own way – but then the proverb says, "A wife should have her will in life because she cannot make one when she dies."

The weather is so warm that I cannot keep rambling much longer, so I'll close with an old- fashioned rhyme:

Heaven bless the wives; they fill our hives
With little bees and honey!
They soothe life's shocks; they mend our socks –
But don't they spend the money!

A Good Word For Wives

"The sign of the Good Woman."

W e pulled up the horses in the last chapter at the sign of the Good Woman, and since there is good hospitality for man, if not for beast, under that sign, we'll stay a while and dip our pen into some of that rare ink that writes without bitterness. When he writes on so fair a subject, John Ploughman must be on his best behavior.

It is astonishing how many old sayings are stacked against wives – you can find nineteen for every dozen. In years gone by, men seemed to show the rough side of their tongues whenever they spoke of their spouses. Some of these sayings are downright cruel, like the wicked one that says, *Every man has two good days with his wife: the day he marries her and the day he buries her*, or the other that claims, *He who loses his wife and a farthing has a great loss of the farthing.*

I remember an old ballad that Gaffer Brooks used to sing about a man's being better off hanged than married. It shows how common it was to abuse married life. It is almost too bad to print it, but here it is, as near as I remember it:

> *There was a victim in a cart,*
> *One day for to be hanged,*
> *And his reprieve was granted,*
> *And the cart made for to stand.*
>
> *"Come marry a wife, and save your life,"*
> *The judge aloud did cry.*
> *"Oh, why should I corrupt my life?"*
> *The victim did reply.*
>
> *"For here's a crowd of every sort,*
> *And why should I prevent their sport?*
> *The bargain's bad in every part,*
> *The wife's the worst – drive on the cart."*

Now this rubbish does not prove that women are bad – it only shows that some men are good for nothing or else they would not make up such abominable slanders about their partners. The rotten branch cracks first, and it looks as if the male side of the house was the worse of the two, for it certainly has made up the most slanderous proverbs. There have, no doubt, been some shockingly bad wives in the world, bad enough to make a man say:

> *If a woman were as little as she is good,*
> *A pea pod would make her a gown and a hood.*

But how many thousands have been true helpmeets, worth far more than their weight in gold! There is only one Job's wife mentioned in the Bible and one Jezebel, but there is no end of Sarahs and Rebekahs. I'm with Solomon: *He who finds a wife finds a good thing* (Proverbs 18:22). If there's one bad shilling taken at the grocery store, all the neighbors will hear of it, but no one says a word about all the good ones. A good woman makes no noise, and no noise is made about her; but a shrew is known all over the parish. All in all, they are most angelic creatures – and too good for half the husbands.

It speaks well of women that there are very few old sayings against husbands, although, in this case, sauce for the goose would make great sauce for the gander, and the mare has as good reasons for kicking as the horse has. They must be very forbearing – or they would have returned fire a long time ago. They may be rather quick in their talk, but is it not the nature of bells and belles to have tongues that swing easy? They cannot be so bad or they would have had their revenge for the many cruel things that are said against them. And if they are a bit masterful, their husbands cannot be very great victims or they would surely have sense enough to hold their tongues about it. Men don't care to have it known when they are thoroughly well henpecked, and I feel pretty certain that the old sayings are nothing but chaff, for if they were true, men would never dare to admit it.

A true wife is her husband's better half, his joy and comfort, his beauty, his guardian angel, and his heart's treasure. He says to her, "I will be happy and rejoice in you. You are my contentment and my blessing." In her company, he finds his earthly heaven. She is the light of his home, the comfort of his soul, and (for this world) the soul of his comfort. If he has her, he is rich as long as she lives. His rib is the best bone in his body.

> *The man who weds a loving wife,*
> *Whate'er betides him in this life,*
> *Shall bear up under all.*
> *But he who finds an evil mate,*
> *No good can come within his gate,*
> *His cup is filled with gall.*

A good husband makes a good wife. Some men can't do with a wife nor without one. They are miserable bachelors and even worse husbands. They are like

Tompkin's dog: He howled when he was tied up and he howled when he was free. Happy bachelors are likely to be happy husbands, and a happy husband is the happiest of men. A well-matched couple will carry a joyful life between them, as the two spies carried the cluster of Eshcol (Numbers 13:23). They are a pair of birds of Paradise. They multiply their joys by sharing them and lessen their troubles by dividing them. That is real arithmetic. The wagon of care rolls lightly along as they pull together, and when it drags a little heavily or there's a hitch anywhere, they love each other all the more and so lighten the labor.

Poverty generally rides home on the husband's back.

When couples quarrel, there's usually fault on both sides – and generally there is a pound on one side and sixteen ounces on the other. A miserable home is just as often the husband's fault as the wife's. If a man won't keep sugar in the cupboard, he shouldn't be surprised if his wife gets sour. Hunger makes love go lean, and lean dogs fight. Poverty generally rides home on the husband's back, for the woman does not often go out working for wages.

A man down our way gave his wife a ring with this on it, "If you don't work, you won't eat." He was a brute. It is not her job to bring in the flour. She is to see it is well used and not wasted; therefore, I say, the scanty food supply is not her fault. She is the bread maker, not the breadwinner. She earns more at home than any wage she can get elsewhere.

It is not the wife who smokes and drinks away the wages at the Brown Bear or the Jolly Topers. A drunk woman is a sad sight, but in ninety-nine cases out of a hundred, it is the man who comes home tipsy and abuses the children – the woman seldom does that. The poor wife is often a teetotaler, whether she likes it or not, and gets plenty of hot water as well as cold.

Women are criticized for looking so much in the mirror, but that is not as bad a glass as men drown their senses in. The wives do not sit drinking for hours over the taproom fire. The poor souls are shivering at home with the baby, watching the clock (if there is one), wondering when their husbands will come home and crying while they wait. It's a wonder they don't strike.

Some of them are like a fly in a web or a mouse in a cat's mouth. They have to nurse the sick girl, wash the dirty boy, and bear with the crying and noise of the children while his lordship puts on his hat, lights his pipe, and does what he pleases. Or he comes home whenever he wants and finds fault with his wife for not having a fine supper ready for him. How can he expect to be fed like a king when he brought home such little money on Saturday night and spent so much in worshipping Sir John Barleycorn?

In many houses there would be no scolding wife if there was not a skulking, guzzling husband. Fellows not fit to be cut up for mops drink and drink until all is blue and then turn on their poor wives for not having more to give them. I have said it, and I will say it again – a woman can't help being irritated when, with all her mending and striving, she can't keep house because her husband won't let her. It would provoke any of us if we had to make bricks without straw, keep the pot boiling without fire, and pay the piper out of an empty purse. What can she get out of the oven when she has neither meal nor dough? You bad husbands, you are full-blooded sneaks and ought to be hung up by your heels until you know better.

They say, *A man of straw is worth a woman of gold*, but I don't believe it. A man of straw is worth no more than a woman of straw. Let old sayings lie as they like; Jack is no better than Jill, as a rule.

When the husband is wise, the wife is usually gentle, and between them, the old wedding wish is worked out: *One year of joy, another of comfort, and all the rest of contentment.* Where hearts agree, there joy will be. United hearts are only parted by death. They say marriage often ends in misery, but that is often when the man eats all the honey and leaves nothing but moonshine. When they both agree that whatever becomes of the moon they will both keep adding honey, the honeymoon never comes to an end.

When a man dwells under the sign of the Cat's Foot and his face is always scratched, either he did not marry a woman or he is no man himself. If a man cannot take care of himself, his wit must be as scant as the wool of a blue dog. I don't pity most of the men martyrs – most of my pity is for the women. Every herring must hang by its own gill, and every person must account for his own share in family quarrels, but John Ploughman can't bear to see all the blame laid on the women. Whenever a dish is broken, the cat did it, and whenever there is mischief, there's a woman at the bottom of it – those are both lies. There's a why for every wherefore, but the why for disagreements does not always lie with the housekeeper.

Yes, some women have long tongues, but who set them wagging? And if you think women talk too much, just sit in a pub when the men's jaws are well oiled with liquor, and if any living women can talk faster or be more stupid than the men, my name is not John Ploughman.

When I got to this point, in walked our minister. "John," he said, "you've taken on a tough subject, a cut above you. Let me lend you a rare old book to help you over the stile." I thanked him kindly, and he sent down William Secker's *The Wedding Ring*. Secker was a real wise fellow, and I picked out a few of his sayings. They are rich and likely to stick in your memory:

Do you have a soft heart? It is of God's breaking. Do you have a sweet wife? She is of God's making. The Hebrews have a saying, "He is not a man who does not have a woman." Though man alone may be good, it is not good for man to be alone. *Every good gift and every perfect gift is from above* (James 1:17). A wife, though she is not a perfect gift, is a good gift, a beam from the Sun of mercy. How happy are those marriages where Christ is at the wedding! Let only those who have found favor in God's eyes find favor in yours. Husbands should spread a cloak of charity over their wives' infirmities. Do not put out the candle because the wick is burnt.

Husbands and wives should provoke one another to love, and they should love one another even if there are irritations. The tree of love should grow up in the midst of the family as the tree of life grew in the garden of Eden. Good servants are a great blessing. Good children a greater blessing. But a good wife is the greatest blessing. Let a man look for her who needs one, let him sigh for her who has lost one, and let him delight in her that enjoys one.

To come down from the old Puritan's roast beef to my own humble herbs, I will close with my own experience.

My first wife, who I hope will live to be my last, is the joy of my days. Marriage came from Eden, and it leads back there. I never was half so happy before I was a married man as I am now. When you are married, your bliss begins. I have no doubt that where there is much love there will be much to love, and where love is scant, faults will be plentiful. If there is only one good wife in England, I am the man who put the ring on her finger, and long may she wear it. God bless the dear soul if she can put up *with* me. She will never be put down *by* me.

If I were single today and saw a suitable partner, I would marry her tomorrow morning before breakfast. What do you think of that? "Well," says one, "I think John would get a new wife if he were left a widower." What if I did? How could I better show that I was happy with my first?

I would not say, as some do, that I married to have someone to look after the children – I married to have someone look after me. John Ploughman is a sociable soul and would not do well in a house by himself.

One man, when he married his fourth wife, put on the ring and said, "If I survive, I'll make it five." What an old Bluebeard! Marriages are made in heaven. Matrimony in itself is good, but there are fools who turn meat into poison and make a blessing into a curse. "This is a good rope – I'll hang myself with it." A man who has sought his wife from God and married her for her character and not merely for her figure, may look for a blessing on his choice. Those who join their love in God above, who pray to love and love to pray, will find that love and joy will never spoil.

He who respects his wife will find that she respects him. With the same measure he uses, it will be measured back to him again; good measure, pressed down, and running over (Luke 6:38). He who consults his spouse will have a good counselor. I have heard our minister say, "Women's instincts are often truer than man's reason." They jump at a thing at once and are wise without even thinking. Say what you will of your wife's advice, it's as likely as not you will be sorry you did not take it.

He who speaks ill of women should remember the breast that nursed him and be ashamed of himself. The man who mistreats his wife ought to be whipped. I'd like a cut at him, and I would make sure it stung. But for now, as the thatcher said when he had cleared every dish on the table – "No more at present."

Men of Two Faces

"Drink or drone will be, as the case may be."

Even dishonest men like to praise consistency. Thieves like honest men because they are the easiest to rob. At least when you know where a man stands, he has one point in his favor. But nobody says a good word about the fellow who howls with the wolves and bleats with the sheep, unless, perhaps, the devil does.

But carrying two faces under one hat is very common. Many roost with the poultry and then go share with the fox. They act as if butter would not melt in their mouths, but they'll breathe fire when it suits their purpose. I saw an ad the other day for reversible coats. The tailor who sells them must be making a fortune. The world is full of people who hold with the hare and run with the hounds. Consistency is about as scarce as perfume in a dog kennel.

Consistency is about as scarce as perfume in a dog kennel.

You can trust some men as far as you can see them, but no further, for when they are in a new crowd, they become brand new people. Like water, they boil or freeze according to the temperature. Some do this because they have no principles. They're like weather vanes and turn with the wind. It would be easier to measure the moon for a suit than to figure out what they are.

They believe in whatever pays best. Their favorite inn is the Golden Fleece. Their mill grinds any kind of grain as long as the money is forthcoming. North wind, south wind, east wind, southwest by south wind, or any other kind of wind – it's all the same. Like frogs, they can live on land or water, and they are fine either way. Like cats, they always land on their feet and will stop anywhere if you butter their paws. They love their friends dearly, but their love lies in the cupboard: if the cupboard is bare, their love, like a mouse, runs off to another pantry. "Leave you, dear girl? Never, while you have a shilling." But if trouble comes, they will vanish. Like rats, they leave a sinking ship.

When good cheer is lacking,
Such friends will be packing.

Their hearts follow the pudding. While the pot's boiling, they sit by the fire. When it's empty and the meal is over, they suddenly disappear. They believe in the winning horse, wear anybody's coat who will give them one, and can be bought by the dozen, like mackerel. But anyone who gives a penny for them is wasting his money. Profit is their god, and whether they make it out of you or your enemy, the money is just as sweet to them. Heads or tails – as long as they win, they're happy. High road or back alley, it makes no difference as long as they go home with a full basket.

They are friends to the goose, but they will eat his giblets. To them, muddy water turns the wheel just as well as clean. They would burn their mother's coffin if they were short of firewood and sell their father's bones if they could make some money. They never miss a chance to mind the main chance.

Others are shifty because they want to be liked. They want to be friends with everyone. "Hello there, friend!" they shout – whether you are a traveler or a thief. They are so good-natured that they will agree with everyone. They are cousins of Mr. Anything. Their brains are in other people's heads. In Rome, they would kiss the pope's toe, but back home, they shout, "No popery!"

They admire the Vicar of Bray, the man who stayed vicar whether the church was Protestant or Catholic. They just wait out their time in hopes that the times may serve them. The palms of their hands are yellow from allowing others to grease their hands. Butter them, and like turnips, you may eat them. Pull the rope, and like bells, they will ring your tune, be it a funeral knell or wedding peal – come to church or go to the devil. They have no backbones. You can bend them forward, backward, or sideways like a willow twig. Like oysters, anyone with a knife can open them and season them as they please. They are sweet to you and sweet to your enemy. They blow hot and cold. They try to be Jack-o'-both sides and deserve to be kicked like a football by both sides.

Some folks are born hypocrites. Slippery as eels and spotted like a piebald horse. Like a drunken man, they could not walk straight if they tried. They wind in and out like a crooked country lane. Their favorite game is the double shuffle. They hate honesty and speak with honey on their lips but gall in their hearts. They are a mix of breeds. Like a cat's feet, they show soft pads, but they carry sharp claws. If their teeth are not rotten, their tongues are. Their hearts are like dead men's graves. If speaking the truth and lying were equally profitable, they'd lie because it comes naturally to them. Like pigs in mud, they delight in deceit.

They fawn and flatter: like snails, they make their way by their slime. But deep down, they hate you and wait for a chance to stab you. Beware the folks from the town of Deceit: Mr. Facing-both-ways, Mr. Fair-speech, and Mr. Two-tongues are neighbors who are best kept at a distance. Like boatmen, they look one way and pull the other. They are as false as the devil's promises and as cruel as death and the grave.

Religious hypocrites are the worst kind of deceivers. I fear they are as plentiful as rats in an old haystack.

They are like a silver pin,
Fair without but foul within.

They cover themselves with white feathers. Saturday night they are one person and Sunday morning, they're another. They fear the minister more than they fear God. Their religion is just mimicry; there is no truth in their hearts. They sing drinking songs while carrying a hymn book in their pocket.

Their Sunday coats are the best part about them. The closer you get to their hearts, the more filth you will find. They prate like parrots, but their talk and their walk do not agree. Some of them are fishing for customers, and a little pious talk is cheap advertising. If the church seat costs them something, they'll make it up by shortchanging and overcharging. They don't worship God while they trade, but they trade on their worship.

Some go to church for soup, bread, and coal tickets. They love the communion because of the alms' money. Some of the dear old Mrs. Goodbodies want a spot in a blessed almshouse, so they profess to be so blessed under the blessed ministry of their blessed Pastor every blessed Sabbath. Charity suits them if faith does not; they know which side their bread is buttered on.

There are those who put on a good religious show to quiet their consciences. Religion is a salve they rub on their guilt. If they could satisfy heaven as easily as they quiet themselves, it would be a fine thing for them.

I have met others who said they were Christians only because they were admired for it. They got some people to believe in their fine talk and take everything they say as gospel. Their opinion was the true measure of a preacher's soundness. They've got gallons of "experience" for those who like something stronger, but if they had just shown a little Christian practice as well, their lives would have mattered more. These people are like owls – they look big, but they are all feathers. They look wise in the twilight, but when the sun shines, you see they are fools.

Hypocrites of all kinds are abominable.

Hypocrites of all kinds are abominable. You will regret dealing with them. Anyone who cheats the Lord will not hesitate to cheat you. All show and no substance. They're big chimneys in which you expect to see bacon and hams, but when you look up, it has nothing to show you but empty hooks and black soot. Their windmills are nutcrackers, and their elephants are baby pigs. Those who sing the loudest are not always the most sincere, and long faces don't always mean godly hearts.

Hypocrites are nasty creatures! Polecats and weasels have nothing on them. It's better to be a dead dog than a live hypocrite. When hypocrites play their little games, it must be as good as a play for the devil. He tempts genuine Christians, but he leaves these alone because he is sure of them. He does not need to shoot at lame ducks – his dog can pick them up any day.

Count on it, friends: if a straight line will not pay, a crooked one certainly won't. What you get by shuffling is very dangerous gain. Wearing a mask may give you a moment's peace, but deception will come home to you and bring sorrow with it. Honesty is the best policy. If the lion's skin doesn't fit, never try the fox's. Be as true as steel. Let your face and hands, like the church clock, always tell how your inner works are going. Better be laughed at as Tom Tell-truth than be praised as Crafty Charlie. Plain dealing might bring trouble, but it is better than shame. The upright will have their reward in the end, but it is as impossible for the double-minded to get to heaven as it is for a man to swim across the Atlantic with a millstone under each arm.

Hints as to Thriving

"If the cat sits long enough at the hole, she
will catch the mouse." – Page 129

Hard work is the great secret to success. Nothing but rags and poverty can come of idleness. The only way to make gold is with elbow grease. No sweat, no sweet. You have to climb the tree to get the crow's eggs. Every man must build his own fortune. Rolled up shirt sleeves lead to dress sleeves, and he who is not ashamed of the apron will soon not need it. "Diligence is the mother of good luck," Poor Richard said. John Ploughman says, "Idleness is the devil's bolster."

Keep moving on, step after step. Don't expect to be rich in a single jump.

Great greediness to reap
Helps not the money heap.

Slow and steady is better than fast and flimsy. Perseverance, with its steady gains, makes a man richer than fits and starts of speculation. Little fish are sweet. Every little bit helps, as the sow said when she snapped at a gnat. A thread a day makes a skein in a year. Houses are built brick by brick. We should crawl before we walk, walk before we run, and run before we ride. On your way to getting rich, the more haste you make, the worse your speed. Haste stumbles over its own feet; hasty climbers have sudden falls.

It's a bad idea to start a business without capital, and you can't shop with empty pockets. You need a nest egg, for hens will lay where there are eggs already. It is true you must bake with the flour you have, but if the flour sack is empty, you might not want to be a baker. Making bricks without straw is easier than making money when you have none to start with. You, young gentleman, stay as a journeyman a little longer. Stay until you have saved a few pounds. Fly when your wings have feathers, but if you try it too soon, you'll end up like the young rook that broke its neck trying to fly before it was fledged. Every minnow wants to be a whale, but it is wise to stay a small fish in a small pond. When your pond becomes the sea, then get as big as you like. Trading without capital is like building a house without bricks, making a fire without sticks, burning candles without wicks. It leads men into tricks and lands them in a fix.

Don't give up a small business until you see that a large one will pay you better. Even crumbs are bread.

Better a poor horse than an empty stall.
Better half a loaf than none at all.

Better a little furniture than an empty house. In hard times, if you can sit on a stone and feed yourself, you better not move. Going from bad to worse is no improvement. A crust is tough fare, but none at all is worse. Don't jump from the frying pan into the fire. Remember, many men have done well in very small shops. A little trade with profit is better than a big one with loss. A small fire that warms you is better than a large fire that burns you. You can get a lot of water from a small pipe if the bucket is always there to catch it. Large hares may be caught in small woods. A sheep may get fat in a small meadow and starve in a huge desert. He who tries to do too much ends up doing little. Two shops are like two stools: you fall to the ground if you are between them. You may burst a bag by trying to fill it too full and ruin yourself by grasping at too much.

In a great river, great fish are found,
But take good heed lest you be drowned.

Make as few changes as you can. Trees that get transplanted often bear little fruit. If you have difficulties in one place, you will have them in another. If you move because it is damp in the valley, you may find it cold on the hill. Where can a donkey go and not have to work? Where can a cow live without being milked? Where is there land without stones or meat without bones? Everywhere on earth men must work to eat bread. You need eagles' wings to fly from trouble. Change isn't always for the better – just ask the pigeon who escaped from the net only to end up in the pie.

Everywhere on earth men must work to eat bread.

Change at the right time, but when you do, get moving. A sitting hen gets no barley. But don't always be shifting – rolling stones gather no moss. Stick-to-it is the conqueror. He who waits long enough will win. This, that, and the other, anything, and everything, all put together make nothing in the end – but riding one good horse will get you home. Seeds grow in one spot, and birds hatch eggs in one nest. Bread bakes in one oven. Fish live in one river.

Don't look down on your own work. A man who turns up his nose at his work quarrels with his bread and butter. Only a poor blacksmith would be afraid of his own sparks. Every job has some discomfort – except maybe chimney sweeping. If sailors stopped going to sea because it's wet, if bakers stopped baking because it's hot, if ploughmen refused to plough because of the cold, and tailors feared a needle prick – where would we all be? Nonsense, my fine fellow! There's no shame in any honest calling. Don't be afraid of getting your hands dirty – there's plenty of soap.

All trades are good to good tradesmen. A clever man can make money out of dirt. Even selling matches pays well if you sell enough of them.

Never mind the stink,
Sweet sounds the chink.

You won't get honey if you're scared of bees. You won't sow corn if you are afraid of getting mud on your boots. Listless gentlemen better emigrate to Fool's-land, where men get their living by wearing shiny boots and lavender gloves. When you can melt iron bars under the south wind, dig fields with toothpicks, blow ships along with fans, manure the crops with lavender water, and grow plum cake in flowerpots, then will be a fine time for dandies. But until the Millennium comes, we all have burdens to bear; and we'd better carry them rather than run headlong into worse ones.

Plod is the word. Everyone must row with the oars he has and sail with the wind God sends him. Patience and attention will win in the long run. If the cat sits long enough at the hole, she will catch the mouse. Always-at-it grows good cabbage and lettuce where others grow thistles. I know as a ploughman that it is up and down, up and down the field that ploughs the acres. You can't cover the ground a mile at a time. He who plods on, clod by clod, will turn up more earth than the lazy man who just nods.

Keep your weather eye open. Sleeping poultry are easy for the fox to catch. Who watches not catches not. Fools ask what time it is, but wise men know their time. Grind while the wind blows – or don't blame providence when the mill stands still. God gives food to the birds, but He does not throw it into the nest. He gives us our daily bread, but we must work for it. Grab time by the forelock. Get up early and catch the worm. The morning hour carries gold in its mouth. He who drives last in line gets all the dust in his eyes. Rise early, and you will have a clear start to the day.

Never stoop to dirty tricks to make money. It never pays to lick honey off thorns. An honest man will not make a dog of himself for the sake of getting a bone. It is hard skating on the devil's ice – you glide fine at first, but it ends in a hard fall and worse. You need a long spoon to eat out of the same dish as Satan. Don't ruin your soul for the sake of dishonest money – it is like drowning yourself in a well to get a drink of water. Do not take on anything that will lead to regret. It is better to walk barefoot than ride in a carriage to hell. Better that the bird go hungry than be fattened for the spit. The mouse gains little by nibbling the cheese if it gets caught in the trap. Clean money or none – mark that well. Ill-gotten gains will be an everlasting loss.

A good product, fair weights, and a just price bring customers back, but people do not recommend the shop where they were cheated. Cheats never thrive; if they do, it is in London, where there are enough visitors to make a living off strangers. The archer who uses the longbow may hit the mark sometimes, but a fair shot is the best. A rogue's purse is full of holes. A man who wears stolen shoes will have blisters on his feet. Sticky fingers pick up more than silver. Steal eels and you will find they turn into snakes. The more a fox robs, the sooner he will be hunted. If a rogue wants to make a good trade, he had better turn honest. Even if you only care about profit, remember that dealing uprightly is the most paying game.

Watch your spending. It doesn't matter what you earn – if you spend more than you make, you will always be poor. The art is not in making money, but in keeping it. Little expenses, like mice in a barn, make great waste. Hair by hair, heads go bald. Straw by straw, thatch disappears, and drop by drop, the roof leaks. A barrel empties fast even if the tap leaks just a drop a minute. Chickens are plucked feather by feather. Tiny mites eat the cheese, and little birds destroy a field of wheat.

Little expenses, like mice in a barn, make great waste.

If you want to save, start with your mouth – there are many thieves down the red lane. The ale jug is a great waster. In all other things, keep within your means. Choose suitable and lasting clothes, not flashy finery. Warmth matters more than looks. Never stretch your legs further than your blankets will reach, or you will soon be cold. A fool may make money, but it takes a wise man to keep it. Remember, it is easier to build two chimneys than to keep one going. If you spend all on food and clothes, there will be nothing left for the savings bank. Live hard and work hard while you are young, and you have a chance of rest when you are old.

Don't live in extravagance unless you want to take a shortcut to the poorhouse. Money has wings of its own, and if you give it another pair of wings, it will fly away fast.

> *He who has it and will not keep it;*
> *He who needs it and will not seek it;*
> *He who drinks and is not dry,*
> *Shall need money as well as I.*

If poor people could see the amount of money they melt away in drink, their hair would stand on end. They swallow rivers of beer, seas of porter, and great big lakes of spirits. We could all dress like gentlemen and live like kings if the money we wasted on alcohol could be sensibly used. We would need to get up earlier in the morning to spend all our money, for we would be rich just from plugging the tap.

At any rate, you young people who want to get ahead – drop your half pints and settle in your spirits that no spirits will ever settle you. Enjoy luxuries, if you must have them, after you have made your fortunes, but for now, focus on your bread and cheese.

Excuse this long yarn, for as I pulled, it came. It's like the Irishman's rope that he could not get into the ship because somebody had cut the end off. I only want to say: Don't be greedy because covetousness is always poor. Strive to get ahead – poverty is no virtue. It is a credit to a man, as well as his comfort, to rise in the world. Earn all you can, save all you can, and then give all you can.

Never try to save by robbing God. That money will rot the rest. Giving to God is never a loss – it is depositing into the best bank. Giving is true having, as the old gravestone said: *What I spent I had, what I saved I lost, what I gave I have.* The pockets of the poor are safe lockers, and lending to the Lord is always a good investment.

John Ploughman wishes all young beginners long life and prosperity:

> *Sufficient of wealth,*
> *And abundant health,*
> *Long years of content,*
> *And when life is spent*
> *A mansion with God in glory.*

Tall Talk

"Gooseberries weigh twice as much as possible." – Page 135

Stretching the truth is commonplace these days. Gooseberries weigh twice as much as possible, and unseen showers of frogs fall regularly when news is slow. If a cart goes by and rattles the lid of an old woman's teapot, it is put down as an earthquake.

Active imaginations are not at all scarce. Certain people are always on the lookout for wonders, and if they don't see them, they invent them. They see comets every night and hear some rare tale every day. All their molehills are mountains. All their ducks are swans.

Active imaginations are not at all scarce.

They have learned the multiplication table and use it freely. If they saw six dogs together, they would swear they saw a hundred hounds and flush with indignation if anybody looked a little doubtful. And before long, they would have convinced themselves they saw ten thousand lions, for everything grows with them as fast as mushrooms and as big as Box Hill.

Everything around them is wonderful – but not nearly as wonderful as they are. There is no one fit to even clean their boots. They are the cream of creation. They are as strong as Samson and could pull against John Ploughman's team – but they won't try it for fear of hurting the horses. Their wealth is enormous – they *could* pay off the national debt, but they have good reasons for not doing so just yet. If they run a shop, they turn over several million a year and only take a break for the sake of their competitors. They sell the best goods at the lowest prices; in fact, they sell them at a loss. No one in the county holds a candle to them. Their business is unmatched. If they have a farm, it is just a hobby and to show the poor, ignorant locals the proper way to do it.

Everything they do is extraordinary! Like the wild beast show that stopped at our village the other day, they are *the only, original, and unrivaled!* But the best part of that show was the pictures outside. It was all a façade. And it's the same with them.

How they stretch the truth! Listen to them talk. It is all in capital letters and sounds of admiration. "Did you ever see SUCH A NAG? Why, sir, it would beat the wind!! THAT COW – let me call your attention to her; there is not another like her in the county. JUST NOTICE THE SWING OF HER TAIL!! Yes, sir, THAT BOY of mine *is* intelligent, far beyond his years. He's a perfect prodigy! *Like his father,* did you say? Very kind remark, sir, but there's a good deal of truth in it. Even though I say it, a man must get up pretty early to get one over on ME! *I'm one too many for most people!*

"Just look over the farm, sir. Was there ever such A FIELD OF TURNIPS? The blight on the leaves? Not a bit, sir; that arises from the peculiar sort. It's A VERY RARE TURNIP, with ventilated leaves pricked through by nature to let the air in and out! Too many moles did you say? Ah! There's a story. Do you know OUR MOLES are quite unique? They throw up bigger hills than any others in England and are supposed to be of a FINE OLD BRITISH STOCK now almost lost.

"Did you notice that TREMENDOUS THISTLE? Is it not a rare specimen? It's enough to make a Scotchman die of joy. That shows the EXTRAORDINARY richness of the soil. Indeed, sir, OUR LAST YEAR'S CROP OF WHEAT was so amazingly heavy, I thought we would never get it home – it nearly broke the wagons. Half the county showed up to see it threshed, and the oldest men in the parish said they never heard anything like it. IT IS A MERCY THAT MACHINES WERE INVENTED – WE NEVER COULD HAVE THRESHED IT BY HAND."

When a man starts yammering like this, no matter what he's going on about, he claims it's the finest, greatest, and most astonishing thing in the kingdom or else the most awful, horrible, and dreadful in the world. His boots would not fit Goliath, but his tongue is much too big for the giant's mouth. He paints with a broom. He sugars his dumpling with a spade and spreads his butter with a trowel. *His* horse, *his* dog, *his* gun, *his* wife, *his* child, *his* singing, *his* planning – there is nothing else like any of them. He is the lead horse of the parish. He lives at Number One, and it would be hard to find a man fit to be number two to him. The water out of his well is stronger than wine. It rains pea soup into his water barrel, his currant bushes grow grapes, and you could live inside one of his pumpkins. His flowers – well, he's heard that the Queen herself had a cutting from that same geranium, but his was the better one! The real marvel is that men of this type don't see that everybody is laughing at them. They must have bragged themselves blind. Everyone sees the bottom of their dish, yet they go on calling it an ocean, as if they only owned flat fish.

I've known men who open their mouths as wide as barn doors to boast about what they would do *if* they were in somebody else's shoes. If they were in Parliament, they would abolish all taxes, turn poor-houses into palaces, make the pumps run with beer, and set the Thames on fire. But it all hinges on an *if,* and that *if* is always some sort of locked gate that keeps him from doing it. If the sky falls, we will catch larks. If Jack Brag gets the reins, he'll make the horses fly up to the moon. *If* is a fine word – if you jump on its back, it will whisk you to worlds that never existed and show you wonders that never happened. With an *if*, you could fit all of London into a quart pot.

> *If all the seas were one sea,*
> *What a great sea that would be!*
> *And if all the trees were one tree,*
> *What a great tree that would be!*
> *And if all the axes were one axe,*
> *What a great axe that would be!*
> *And if all the men were one man,*
> *What a great man he would be!*
> *And if the great man took the great axe,*
> *And cut down the great tree,*
> *And let it fall into the great sea,*
> *What a splash that would be!*

"What nonsense!" you say. John Ploughman agrees, so he adds it as a specimen of the stupidity that tall talkers are so fond of. This is not half as silly as nine out of ten of their lofty ramblings.

You wouldn't believe what some of these fellows claim they've done! They made their own fortunes in no time at all – and made other people's too. Their advice has made many people rich. Their speeches glue people to their seats like cobbler's wax. In a debate, when their side was crumbling, they finished off the opposition with razor-sharp wit and wisdom – King Solomon was a fool to them.

As to religion, they practically founded it in their parish, and their tireless efforts got everything going. They laid the golden egg. People aren't grateful, or they'd be practically worshipped. It's a disgrace how they have been overlooked and even ignored by the very people they have made. While they had a hand in things, everything was going well, but now that they have left, everything's wobbly, and those who live the longest will see the proof.

When they are in a modest humor they borrow words from David, and say, "*The earth and all its inhabitants are dissolved; I set up its pillars firmly* (Psalm 75:3). Their death will leave the world in ruins. If they stop shopping at a store, it's doomed to close immediately, and it is only their impudence that makes them hope they can make a living after such customers are gone. When they're feeling proud at their great deeds, you should hear them talk! Forget blowing your own horn – they have a whole band of music, big drum and all, and keep all the instruments going, blasting their own praises.

I'd rather plough all day and be on the road with the wagon all night in a blizzard than listen to these big talkers; they make me as sick as a cat. I'd sooner go without eating until I was as thin as a rake than eat the best turkey that ever was on a table while they drone on with their nonsense. They talk so big and magnify everything so thunderingly that you cannot believe them when they accidentally slip in a word or two of truth – you start thinking even their gold is glitter.

They are great liars, but they hardly realize it; they have talked themselves into believing their own bluster. The frog thought herself equal to the cow and began to blow herself out to make it true. These people swell like her, and they will burst like her if they aren't careful.

Everybody who knows these big talkers should take heed from their example:

> *Said I to myself, here's a lesson for me,*
> *This man is a picture of what I might be.*

We must try to state the truth, the whole truth, and nothing but the truth. If we begin calling eleven inches a foot, we'll soon stretch one inch into twenty-four. If we call a heifer a cow, we may one day call a dormouse a bull. Once you dabble in exaggeration, you may as well be hung for a sheep as a lamb. You have left the road of truth, and there is no telling where the crooked lane may lead. He who tells little lies will soon think nothing of huge ones, for the principle is the same. Where there's a mouse hole, a rat hole will follow, and if the kitten sneaks in, the cat's not far behind. When it rains, it often pours; a little untruth leads to a perfect shower of lying.

The frog thought herself equal to the cow and began to blow herself out to make it true.

Self-praise is no commendation. A man's praise smells sweet when it comes out of other men's mouths, but from his own, it stinks. Grow your own cherries, but don't sing your own praises.

Boasters aren't worth a button without its shank.

Long tongue, short hand. Great talkers, little doers. Dogs that bark often run away when it is time to bite. The scrawniest pig squeals most. The hen that cackles loudest rarely lays the most eggs. Saying and doing are two different things. It is the barren cow that bellows. You may hear a great noise of threshing where there is no wheat. Great boast, little roast. Much froth, little beer. Drums sound loud because they are empty. Good men know themselves too well to chant their own praises. Barges without cargo float high on the canal, but the fuller they are, the lower they sink. Good cheese sells itself without a lot of advertising, good wine needs no signboard, and when men are truly worthy, people will notice without a word. Boasting is the mark of folly. Loud braying reveals an ass. If a man is ignorant and holds his tongue, no one will scorn him; but if he rattles on with an empty head and a tongue that brags like forty, he will write out his own name in capital letters: F O O L.

> *As by the ears the ass is known –*
> *A truth as sure as parsons preach,*
> *The man, as proverbs long have shown,*
> *Is seen most clearly through his speech.*

Things I Would
Not Choose

"I wouldn't choose to be gossiped to death by sharp-tongued washerwomen." – Page 145

If it were all the same to other folks and I could have things my way, I would not choose to have my humble book pulled to pieces by people who do not have the honesty to read it. They made up their minds beforehand, as Simple Simon did when they put him on the jury. But as the rhinoceros said, I do not have thin skin, so if it amuses others to find fault with me, they are as welcome as they are free.

The anvil does not flinch from the hammer. They tell me those London editors slice a page open, sniff the knife, and then either praise the book up to the skies or rip it to shreds, abusing it without mercy, depending on their whims or what they had for lunch. John Ploughman hopes the publisher will fold down this page when he sends the book to the papers, and he hopes this word to the wise will be enough: I hope my pears don't end up in pigs' mouths.

I would not choose, if I had my druthers, to see these pages wrapping butter the next time we shop, but it's likely enough, so I must put up with it, like Tom Higgs did when stuck with only turkey and plum pudding for dinner.

I would not choose to plough with two old horses, worn and wind-broken and altogether unfit for work. Pity the poor horses, pity the poor ploughman, but do not pity the farmer who keeps such wretched cattle. When I see a man whipping and slashing a poor brute of a horse, I want to kick him, but at the same time, I feel glad that Violet and Dapper move lively at the crack of the whip without needing to be paid like lawyers for all they do. A man who knocks a horse about ought to be put in harness himself and driven about by a butcher. Treat your animals with kindness, not cruelty. He who is unmerciful to his beast is worse than a beast himself.

I wouldn't choose to be a bob-tailed cow in summer, a servant with twenty masters, a minister with six ignorant tyrants for deacons, nor a man who lives with his mother-in-law. Nor would I like to try the truth of the old saying:

> *Two cats and one mouse,*
> *Two women in one house,*
> *Two dogs to one bone,*
> *Will not agree long.*

I'd rather not be a dog with a tin can tied to its tail, a worm on a fisherman's hook, an eel skinned alive, nor a husband with a shrew for a wife. I would much rather not fall into the jaws of a crocodile or the hands of a lawyer – the only suit that lasts too long is a lawsuit, and that would not suit me at all. I wouldn't choose to be gossiped to death by sharp-tongued washerwomen or pestered by a pushy bookseller trying to sell me six-penny installments of a book that will run on forever, like old Jimmy's debts.

I'd be very hard up before I would choose to sleep with pigs or live in some folks' filthy houses. I would not choose to own half the cottages poor workers are forced to live in: no farmer would stable his horses there, and they are not good enough for dog kennels. Imagine a father, mother, grown son, and two daughters all sleeping in the same room! It is a shameful disgrace and a crying sin on the part of those who drive people to such straits. It's unbearable to think of, yet it is all too common. Squires and landlords, how would you like it? If anyone defends such a system, half an hour's hanging would do them good.

To be servant to a miser, to work for a wasp, to be a monkey's wrench, or a lackey to a lord without brains, I would not choose. I do not want to go to the workhouse nor apply for parish relief. I'd sooner try Grantham gruel – nine grits and a gallon of water. I would not beg, hat in hand, for money for my own pocket. I would not choose to borrow money, be a loafer, or live like a toad under a harrow. No, not for all the good that ever thawed out of the cold hand of charity.

Bad off as I am, I would not choose to change unless I could better myself. Who would stand under the spout to get out of the rain? Why travel to the ends of the earth to be worse off than you are? Old England is fine for me, and Botany Bay is for those who want to ship themselves off.

I wouldn't choose to drive a pig, tame a stubborn nag, nor try to reason with a man with a wooden head. I would not like to be a schoolmaster with rowdy boys, a bull baited by dogs, nor a hen who has hatched ducklings. Worse yet is a preacher with drowsy listeners; he's hunting with dead dogs and driving wooden horses. You might as well preach to sleeping swine as to sleeping men.

If I could help it, I would not buy a horse from a horse dealer because no one has ever heard of the two or three honest ones. An "honest" horse dealer won't cheat you if you don't let him; an ordinary one will swipe your eyetooth while your mouth is shut. Horses are nearly as tricky to judge as men's hearts. Even old hands get fooled. What with bone spavin, ringbone, splints, grease, crown scab, rattail, windgalls, cankers, colic, jaundice, sandcracks, founders, mallenders, and sallenders, sound horses are hard to find. It's best not to swap horses at all. If you have a good one, keep it, for you likely won't find better. If you have a bad one, keep it, for ten to one you will buy worse.

I would not choose to be a doormat, a poodle, nor a fellow who will eat dirt in order to curry favor with bigwigs. Others can lie to please the great; I'd rather have truth on my side, even if I go barefoot. Independence and a clear conscience are better with cold cabbage than slavery and sin with roast beef.

I would not like to keep a tollgate at the top of a steep hill, be a tax collector, a summons officer, a general nuisance, nor a poor postman with half enough to live on and twice the work he should have. It would be better to be a gypsy's horse and live on the common with no hay and no oats, just plenty of oak cudgel.

I would not choose to be plucked like a goose, be a shareholder in a company, be fried alive, nor to be at the mercy of a priest.

I would not stand as godfather to anyone's child, vowing the little sinner will keep God's holy commandments and walk in them all the days of his life. I'd sooner promise to put the moon into my coat sleeve and pull it out my trouser leg or vow that the little dear will have red hair and a snub nose. Nor would I let lies be told over my baby to cozy up to the parson's good side to get a Christmas blanket.

I would not choose to go where I would be afraid to die nor live without a good hope for the hereafter. I would not choose to sit on a barrel of gunpowder and smoke a pipe, but that is what those do who ignore their souls while life is so uncertain. I would not choose my lot on earth but leave it to God to choose for me. I might pick and choose the worst, but His choice is always best.

Try

"'We shall get through it now,' said Jack to Harry,
as they fnished up the pudding." – Page 150

Of all the charming little songs I have heard my youngsters sing, one of the best ends with:

If at first you don't succeed,
Try, try, try again.

I recommend it to adults who are discouraged and sad and imagine that the best thing they can do is to give up. Nobody knows what he can do until he tries. "We'll get through it now," said Jack to Harry as they finished up the pudding. Everything new is hard work, but a little of the *TRY* ointment, rubbed on the hand and worked into the heart, makes all things easier.

Can't-do-it sticks in the mud, but Try drags the wagon out of the rut. The fox said, "Try," and escaped the hounds nipping at his heels. The bees said, "Try" and turned flowers into honey. The squirrel said, "Try" and scampered to the top of the beech tree. The snowdrop said "Try" and bloomed in the cold snows of winter. The sun said, "Try," and the spring soon threw Jack Frost out of the saddle. The young lark said, "Try," and he found that his new wings took him over hedges and ditches and up to where his father was singing. The ox said, "Try" and ploughed the field from end to end. No hill is too steep for Try to climb, no clay too stiff for Try to plough, no field too wet for Try to drain, no hole too big for Try to mend.

> *By little strokes*
> *Men fell great oaks.*

A spadeful at a time, the workers dug through the hills and raised the embankments.

> *The stone is hard, and the drop is small,*
> *But a hole is made by the constant fall.*

What one person has done, another can too – and what has never been done might still be. Ploughmen have risen to prominence, shoemakers have built fortunes, and tailors have become government leaders. Roll up your sleeves, young dreamer, and dive in. Where there's a will, there's a way. The sun shines for everyone. Believe

Every man must carry his own load.

in God, stick to hard work, and watch the mountains be removed. Faint hearts never win fair ladies. Forget luck; that's what the fool had when he killed himself by indulging in suet pudding. The best luck in all the world is made up of faith first, but our part in it requires good old effort and perseverance.

Don't wait for help. Try those two old friends, your strong arms. If the fox wants poultry for his cubs, he must carry the chickens home himself. The hare's friends can't help her; she has to outrun the dogs by herself. Every man must carry his own load. Put you shoulder to the wheel and keep it there – the road is full of ruts. If you wait for perfect paths, you will have light shining between your ribs. If you sit waiting for others to carry you, you will grow to your seat. Your own legs are better than stilts. Don't look to others; trust God and keep your powder dry.

Don't whine about not having a fair start. If you throw a sensible man out of a window, he'll land on his feet and ask the nearest way to his work. The more you have to begin with, the less you will have at the end. Money you earn yourself is much brighter and sweeter than any you inherit. A scant breakfast in the morning of life whets the appetite for a feast later in the day.

Eating a sour apple makes you enjoy a sweeter one even more. Your current need will make future prosperity all the sweeter. A small sum has given many peddlers a start, and they kept making profits until they became successful businessmen.

Don't find fault with your circumstances. You do not need to be a horse because you were born in a stable. If a bull tossed a determined man sky high, he would drop down into a good place. A hardworking young man, with his wits about him, will make money where others do nothing but lose it.

> *Who loves his work and spends with care,*
> *May live and flourish anywhere.*

As for a few challenges, who expects to find cherries without stones or roses without thorns? To win, you must endure. Idleness lies in bed festering in complaints while industry finds health and wealth. The dog in the kennel barks at the fleas; the hunting dog does not even know they are there. Laziness waits until the river is dry and never gets to market; Try swims it and seizes all the business. Can't-do-it couldn't eat the bread and butter that was cut and handed to him, but Try made meat out of mushrooms.

Some blame failure on competition. When the wine was stolen, they said it was the rats. It's very convenient to have a horse to put the saddle on. A mouse may find a hole even if the room is full of cats. Good workmen are always wanted. You can make a penny even at the worst booth in the fair. No barber ever shaves so close that another barber can't find something left. Nothing is so good that it can't be made better, and he who sells the best wins the trade.

The prophets down at the pub told us we were all going to the workhouse because of the new machines, but instead, all these threshing, reaping, and haymaking machines have helped to make those men better off who had sense enough to work them. If a man is content to be backward, he may expect to keep poor,

Many falter because they don't have the courage to start strong.

but if he opens his head and picks up here a little and there a little, even Johnny Raw may progress. "Times are bad," they say; yes, and if you move aimlessly about and send your wits daydreaming, times always will be bad.

Many falter because they don't have the courage to start strong. The first saving is the hardest. The first blow is half the battle. Put down the beer mug, and put up the Try flag. Get out to your work and then to the bank with your savings – and you will be a man yet.

Poor men will always be poor if they think they must always be. But there's a way out of the lowest poverty if a man acts early, before he has a wife and half-a-dozen children. After that, he carries too much weight for racing and must usually be content just having enough to feed and clothe his children. Yet, some hens scratch even better because they have a great swarm of chicks. The road up the hill may be steep for young men, but it is open. Those who firmly set their hearts to get up that hill will climb it.

What was hard to bear will be sweet to recall. If young men deny themselves, work hard, live hard, and save in their early days, they do not need to keep their noses to the grindstone all their lives, as many do. Let them be teetotalers to save money. Water is the strongest drink. It drives mills. It's the drink of lions and horses, and Samson never drank anything else. The beer money would soon build a house.

If you want to do good in the world, the little word *Try* comes in again. There are plenty of ways to serve God, and some will fit you exactly as a key fits a lock. Don't hold back because you cannot preach in St. Paul's Cathedral. Be content to talk to one or two in a cottage; very good wheat grows in little fields. You can cook in small pots as well as in big ones. Little pigeons can carry great messages. Even a little dog can bark at a thief, wake up the master, and save the house. A spark can start a fire. A sentence of truth has heaven in it. Do your work well, pray over it sincerely, and leave the result to God.

Sadly, advice is thrown away on some, like good seed on a bare rock. You can teach a cow for seven years, but she will never learn to sing a hymn. When some people were born, Solomon walked by the doorway but did not look in. Their coat of arms is a fool's cap on a donkey's head. They sleep when it is time to plough then weep when harvest comes. They eat all the parsnips for supper and are surprised they have none left for breakfast. Our working people are shamefully wasteful, and so old England swarms with the poor. If the money that was spent making beer went into making bread, families would be better fed and better taught. If the money that is wasted were saved for a rainy day, workhouses would never be built.

If every man said "Try,"
Very few on straw would lie;
Fewer still of want would die.
Pans would all have fish to fry,
Pigs would fill the poor man's sty;
Want would cease and need would fly.
Wives and children cease to cry,
Poor rates would not swell so high;
Things wouldn't go so much awry –
You'd be glad, and so would I.

Monuments

"Some men are hardly better than walking beer barrels while they live." – Page 158

Every man should leave behind a monument in the memory of his neighbors by the life he lived. There must be something deeply wrong with a man who is not missed when he dies. A good character is the best tombstone. Those who loved you and were helped by you will remember you long after the forget-me-nots have wilted. Carve your name on hearts, not on marble. Live in such a way that others will keep your memory alive when the grass grows on your grave.

Let us hope something better will be said about us than was written of the man whose epitaph read:

> *Here lies a man who did no good,*
> *And if he'd lived, he never would.*
> *Where he's gone and how he fares,*
> *Nobody knows, and nobody cares.*

And may our friends never remember us as gluttons, like the man over whose grave is written:

> *Gentle reader, gentle reader,*
> *Look on the spot where I do lie,*
> *I always was a very good feeder,*
> *But now the worms do feed on I.*

That might have been said of a prize pig or a fat ox that died of some disease. Some men are hardly better than walking beer barrels while they live; when death breaks open the cask, they deserve to rot in obscurity.

Still, a plain and honest tombstone is better than downright lying. Flattering the dead is like pouring melted butter down a stone sink. What strange tastes people must have who puff up the departed as though they were blowing the trumpet of the dead before the last angel arrives. Here's a sample of their nonsense:

Here lies the body of Martha Gwyn,
Who was so very pure within;
She cracked the outer shell of sin,
And hatched herself a cherubim.

Where do they bury all the bad people? Those buried in our churchyard all seem to have been the best of folks, a regular nest of saints. Some of them so precious good, it is no wonder they died – they were too pure to live in such a wicked world as this. It's better to give bread to the poor than stones to the dead – and better to speak kindly to the living than make fancy speeches over their graves. Some of the overdone stuff on monuments is enough to make a dead man blush.

What heaps of marble are stuck over the graves of the great! Enough to build a house with! What a heavy load they will have to lift at the resurrection! Just thinking of all those stones pressing down on me makes me short of breath – not that I need to worry about that. Let the same earth that I have turned over so often lie light upon me when I am laid beneath it. Bury John Ploughman somewhere under the boughs of a spreading beech, with a green grass mound above him, where primroses and daisies bloom in season – a quiet shady spot where the leaves fall, robins play, and the dew sparkles in the morning sun. Let the wind blow fresh and free over my grave, and if there must be a line about me, let it be this:

HERE LIES THE BODY OF
JOHN PLOUGHMAN,

WAITING FOR THE APPEARING OF HIS LORD AND SAVIOR, JESUS CHRIST

I've often heard of patience on a monument, but I have never seen it sitting there when I have walked through churchyards. I *have* seen plenty of stupidity on monuments and wondered why the parson, the churchwarden, or the sexton allow such rubbish to be carved in stone. Why, a fellow from Gloucestershire told me that in Dymock graveyard there's a gravestone that reads like this:

> *Too sweetur babes you nare did see*
> *Than God amity gave to wee;*
> *But they wur ortaken wee agur fits,*
> *And hear they lys has dead as nits.*

I've read nearly enough silly things on tombstones in our Surrey burial grounds to fill a book. Better leave the grave unmarked than to erect a monument to your own ignorance.

Of all places for jokes, tombstones are the strangest, yet many times, gravestones have such oddities carved on them that one would think the closer you are to the church, the further you are from common decency. This is a cruel verse, but likely true:

> *Here lies, returned to clay,*
> *Miss Arabella Young,*
> *Who on the first of May*
> *Began to hold her tongue.*

This is not much better:

> *John Adams lies here, of the parish of Southwell,*
> *A carrier who carried his can to his mouth well.*
> *He carried so much, and he carried so fast,*
> *He could carry no more, so was carried at last.*
> *For the liquor he drunk was too much for one,*
> *He could not carry off, so he's now carri-on.*

Couldn't they have found someplace else for their humor? A man's wit must be nearly dead when he can find no place for it but the grave. Even the body of the poorest beggar is too sacred for mockery. What kind of character must Roger Martin of Walworth have been to have put this on his wife's tomb:

> *Here lies the wife of Roger Martin,*
> *She was a good wife to Roger – that's sartin.*

And who was the fool in Ockham, one of the prettiest spots around here, who wrote these outrageous lines?

> *The Lord saw good, I was topping off wood,*
> *And down fell from the tree.*
> *I met with a check, and I broke my blessed neck,*
> *And so death topped off me.*

That's enough of that. It is proof positive that some fools are left alive to write nonsense on the graves of the dead. There just may be ghosts around – the sleepers get out of bed when they have been so poorly tucked in. I say we ought not allow a person to write nonsense over the dead unless he has a certificate to be an ass, just like a license to shoot partridges and pheasants. Save your puffery for drapers' shops and quack doctors – don't bring it to the cemetery.

As our minister rightly says:

> *Let no proud stone with sculptured virtues rise,*
> *To mark the spot wherein a sinner lies,*
> *Or if some boast must deck the sinner's grave,*
> *Boast of His love who died, lost man to save.*

One more Surrey rhyme, and John Ploughman will leave the churchyard to go back to his work turning up the sod. It is in St. Saviour's, Southwark, and I think it's a rare good one:

> *Like to the damask rose you see,*
> *Or like the blossom on the tree,*
> *Or like the dainty flow'r of May,*
> *Or like the morning of the day,*
> *Or like the sun or like the shade,*
> *Or like the gourd which Jonah had;*
> *Even so is man, whose thread is spun,*
> *Drawn out and cut and so is done.*
> *The rose withers, the blossom blasteth,*
> *The flower fades, the morning hasteth,*
> *The sun sets, the shadow flies,*
> *The gourd consumes, and man he dies.*

Very Ignorant People

"The fox admires the cheese, not the raven." – Page 169

I have heard of a man who did not know a capital "A" from a bull's foot, and I know a good many who certainly could not tell you what either capital "A" or little "a" means. But even some of these people are not the most ignorant in the world.

For instance, they know a cow's head from its tail – something a London political candidate apparently couldn't manage, according to one of the locals. They know that turnips don't grow on trees, they can tell a mangelwurzel from a beetroot and a rabbit from a hare. Yet there are fine folks who play on pianos who don't know even that much.

Perhaps they cannot read, but they can plough, mow, reap, sow, and bring up seven children on ten shillings a week – and still pay their way. There are plenty of educated people who are not able to do that. Not knowing how to spell is bad, but knowing nothing about hard work is worse. Wisdom does not always speak Latin. People laugh at the clothes farm workers wear, and indeed, they are ugly – but some who wear them are far from fools. If only the ignorant people who wear hobnail shoes ate bread, the price of corn would be far lower. Wisdom in a poor man is like a diamond set in lead – not many recognize its worth. Wisdom often walks in patched clothes, and then no one admires her. But I say – never mind the coat; give me the man. The shell is nothing; the kernel is what counts.

You do not need to go all the way to Pirbright to find ignoramuses, there are heaps of them near St. Paul's.

I'd like everyone to learn to read, write, and do arithmetic – I don't think a man can know too much. But let's be clear: knowing these things is not the same as being educated. There are millions of people who can read and write but are as ignorant as neighbor Norton's calf that didn't know its own mother.

This is as plain as the nose on your face if you stop

to think: learning to read and write is like having tools – but if you don't use those tools or your eyes and ears either, you're no better off. Everyone ought to know what most concerns him and makes him most useful.

Cats can catch mice, and hens can lay eggs – they are doing what they were made to do. A horse doesn't need to know how to fly – it will do just fine if it can trot. A farmhand should know farming, a blacksmith should study a horse's foot, a dairymaid should be skilled in skimming the milk and making the butter, and a laborer's wife should be an expert in the sciences of boiling, baking, washing, and mending.

Girls are taught dancing and French when stitching and English would be ten times more useful.

John Ploughman dares to say that anyone – man or woman – who hasn't learned the duties of his calling is a very ignorant person, even if he knows the Greek name for a crocodile or can write a poem about a black beetle. Too often it proves true:

Jack has been to school
To learn to be a fool.

If a man falls into the water, knowing how to swim will be of more use to him than all his mathematics – and yet how very few boys learn swimming! Girls are taught dancing and French when stitching and English would be ten times more useful. These are hard times. A solid trade and good work habits are worth more than all the classics in Cambridge and Oxford, but who advocates for practical training in our schools these days? Schoolmasters would have fits if they were asked to teach poor people's boys to hoe potatoes and plant cauliflower, yet school boards would be doing something good if they did something like that.

If you want a dog to be a pointer or a setter, you train him accordingly – why don't they do the same with men? It should be *every man for his calling, and every man master of it.* By all means, let Jack and Tom learn geography, but don't forget to teach them how to polish their own boots and sew on a button. As for Jane and Sally, let them sing and play the music if they like – but not until they know how to darn a sock and make a shirt.

When they revise that Education Act, I hope they add a clause to teach children practical common-sense home duties – along with the three Rs. But then again, what's the use of talking this way, for where would we find the teachers who can teach common sense? Very few people have any of it to spare, and those who do wouldn't likely go into teaching.

Many girls learn nothing except frills, which I think they call "accomplishments." Poor Mr. Gent – six girls and only fifty pounds a year to support them. But not one of them can lift a finger to help because their mother would go into fits lest Miss Sophia Elfrida should have chapped hands from washing the family linen or lest Alexandra Theodora should spoil her complexion in picking a few gooseberries for a pudding.

It's enough to make a cat laugh to hear the poor things talk about fashion and etiquette when they are not half as well off as the peddler's daughters down the lane, who earn their own living and are saving up for the day when some young farmer comes courting. Trust me, if a man marries one of these fancy misses, he might as well marry a wax doll. Mrs. Gent would have a fit if she heard me say it, but I say it anyway – she and her girls are *ignorant, very ignorant,* because they do not know what would actually help them in life.

Every sprat now calls itself a herring. Every donkey thinks it ought to be one of the Queen's horses. Every candle thinks it is the sun. But when a man struts about in his best coat, with a paper collar, a monocle in his eye, a brass chain on his waistcoat, a cane in his hand, and nothing in his head – thinking he is fooling everyone – he must be *ignorant, very ignorant,* because he doesn't even know himself. These naïve people, dressed up to the top of the fashion, think themselves somebodies, but nobody else does. You can dress up a fool and teach him to dance, but you cannot make him into a man. You can paint a millstone as much as you like, but you cannot turn it into cheese.

Every donkey thinks it ought to be one of the Queen's horses.

Round our way, we have a lot of poets – at least a bunch of *very ignorant* people who think they are. These folks bother me to no end. They think that because I have written a book, I must want to listen to their nonsense. Nonsense is nonsense whether it rhymes or not, just as bad halfpennies are worthless whether they jingle or lie quiet. One fellow came up to me and said, "Here, John, I want to read you some of my verses."

"No, thank you," I said. "I don't feel in a poetical frame of mind today." Truth be told, I won't tomorrow either. What gives him the right to dump his rubbish at my door? I have enough of my own. I don't intend to have my ears stuffed up with cobbler's wax or cobbled verses.

I had a double dose the other morning from two of our great village poets, and I must admit it was better than most of the rhymes that I read in books. Chubbins said:

"It is a sin to steal a pin,"

And Padley topped it up by adding,

"It is a greater to steal a tater."

Now, there's rhyme and reason for you, as the sexton said when he wrote three lines for the poor man's tombstone:

Here I lie,
Killed by a sky-
Rocket in my eye.

When tradesmen put their earnings into risky companies and expect to see it again or when they lend money at outrageous interest hoping to make a fortune, they must be *ignorant, very ignorant*. You might as well hang a wooden kettle over the fire to boil the water for tea or sow beans in a river and look for a fine crop.

When men believe in lawyers and moneylenders, borrow money, gamble with it and think they are lucky, they are shamefully *ignorant.* Even the goose on the village common wouldn't fall for such nonsense, for he knows when someone is trying to pluck him and won't lose his feathers and boast about it while it is happening.

The man who spends his money at the pub and thinks that the landlord's bows and "How are you, my good fellow?" mean true respect is a perfect simpleton. For their motto is:

> *If you have money, take a seat.*
> *If you have none, take to your feet.*

The fox doesn't flatter the raven because he cares about him but because he wants the cheese. The bait is not put into the trap to feed the mouse but to catch him. Fires aren't lit for the herring's comfort but to roast him for dinner.

Men do not keep taverns for the good of the working man; if they do, they certainly miss their mark. Why, then, should people *drink for the good of the house*? If I spend money for the good of any house, let it be my own, not the landlord's. It's a bad well that needs you to pour water into it before you can draw some out – and the beerhouse is that kind of well. It takes your all and leaves you with nothing but dregs and headaches. The fellow who calls those his friends who let him sit and drink by the hour together is *ignorant, very ignorant.* Red Lions, Tigers, Eagles, and Vultures – pub names as they may be – are all creatures of prey, and only fools wander willingly into their jaws and talons.

He who believes that either party of government

will let us off with light taxes must have been born on the day after the last of March. And the one who imagines that parish boards and councils will ever be free from those in it to feather their own nests must have been educated in an idiot asylum. The voter who believes election promises has long ears and may try to eat thistles. Mr. Plausible comes around asking all the working men for their votes, promising to do all sorts of good things for them. Will he? Yes, the day after tomorrow – a little later than never. Poor men who expect the "friends of the working man" to do anything for them must be *ignorant, very ignorant.* When they get their seats, they cannot stand up for their principles except when it is to their own interest to do so.

Relying on others has ruined many.

To lend umbrellas and expect them back, to do a man a good turn and expect another from him when you want it, to dream of stopping some women's gossip, to try to please everybody, to hope to hear gossips speak well of you, or to count on getting the truth from a town rumor are all evidences of great ignorance. Those who know the world best trust it least. Trusting it at all is unwise; you'd do just as well to trust a horse's kick or a dog's bite!

Relying on others has ruined many. A man who leaves his business to hired hands and thinks it will be run smoothly must be *ignorant, very ignorant.* The mouse knows when the cat is out of the house, and the servants know when the master is away. The minute the boss turns his back, the worker's hand slows down – at least, in nine times out of ten. "I'll go myself" and

"I'll see to it" are two of the best farmhands you'll ever have. Those who lie in bed and tell themselves that their trade will carry on itself are *ignorant, very ignorant.*

Those who drink and live riotously and then wonder why their faces are so blotchy and their pockets so bare would stop wondering if they had an ounce of sense. Those who go to the pub for happiness climb a tree to find fish. You could fit all their wisdom into an eggshell. If they had more sense, they would not hunt after comfort where it is no more to be found than a cow in a crow's nest.

But sadly, good-for-nothings are as common as mice in a haystack. If someone could let loose fellows see the certain result of ill-living, perhaps they might reform; yet I don't know, for they do see it and keep on going, like a moth that burns its wings in the flame and dashes into the candle again. If lazy drinkers expect to prosper with their hands in their pockets or their noses in pewter mugs, they're *ignorant, very ignorant.*

When I see a young lady with a flower garden on her hat and a draper's shop on her body, tossing her head as if she thought everybody was charmed with her, I am sure she is *ignorant, very ignorant.* Sensible men don't want to marry a wardrobe or a hatbox; they want a woman of sense, and those women do not dress gaudily.

Fellows who sneer at religion and act like they are too clever to believe in the Bible are shallow souls. They use big words and boast a great deal, but if they think they can overturn the faith of thinking people who have tried and proved the power of the grace of God, they must be *ignorant, very ignorant.* A man who can watch the sun rise and the sun set and does not see the footprints of God must be inwardly blinder than a mole and only fit to live underground. God seems to talk to me in every primrose and daisy, to smile on me from every star, to whisper to me in every breath of morning air, and to call aloud to me in every storm.

It is strange that so many educated gentlemen do not see God anywhere, while John the ploughman feels Him everywhere. John has no wish to change places, for the sense of God's presence is his comfort and joy. They say that man is the god of the dog – well, those men who refuse to listen to the voice of God must be worse than dogs, for a dog obeys its master's whistle. They call themselves "philosophers," don't they? Their proper name is fools, for *the fool has said in his heart, "There is no God"* (Psalm 14:1). The sheep can sense when rain is coming, the swallows know when winter's near, and even the pigs, they say, can tell which way the wind blows. But what brute is worse than a man who lives in a world where God is present everywhere but never sees Him?

So, it is plain enough – a man may be learned in books and still be *ignorant, very ignorant.*

Other Similar Titles

Morning by Morning
by Charles H. Spurgeon

Charles H. Spurgeon's devotionals *Morning by Morning* and *Evening by Evening* have inspired, encouraged, and challenged Christians for generations. Spurgeon, with his masterful hand, carefully selected his text from throughout the Bible and covered a broad range of topics, in order to present a well-balanced and fruitful daily devotional for readers both young and old.

Now updated into more-modern English for today's readers, and again separated into two volumes as originally published, with morning devotionals in one volume and evening devotionals in the second. We chose a 11-point font for the sake of legibility, and formatted the devotionals so each fits on a single page.

Available where books are sold

Faithful to Christ
by Charles H. Spurgeon

I believe that many Christians get into a lot of trouble by not being honest in their convictions. For instance, if a person goes into a workshop, or a soldier into a barracks, and if he does not fly his flag from the beginning, it will be very difficult for him to run it up afterwards. But if he immediately and boldly lets them know, "I am a Christian, and there are certain things that I cannot do to please you, and certain other things that I cannot help doing even though they might displease you" – when that is clearly understood, after a while the peculiarity of the thing will be gone, and the person will be let alone.

However, if he is a little dishonest and thinks that he is going to please the world and please Christ too, he can depend on it that he is in for a rough time. If he tries the way of compromise, his life will be like that of a toad under a harrow or a fox in a dog kennel. That will never do. Come out. Show your colors. Let it be known who you are and what you are. Although your course will not be smooth, it will certainly not be half as rough as if you tried to run with the hare and hunt with the hounds, which is a very difficult piece of business.

Available where books are sold

9 7 9 8 8 8 9 3 6 5 2 9 7